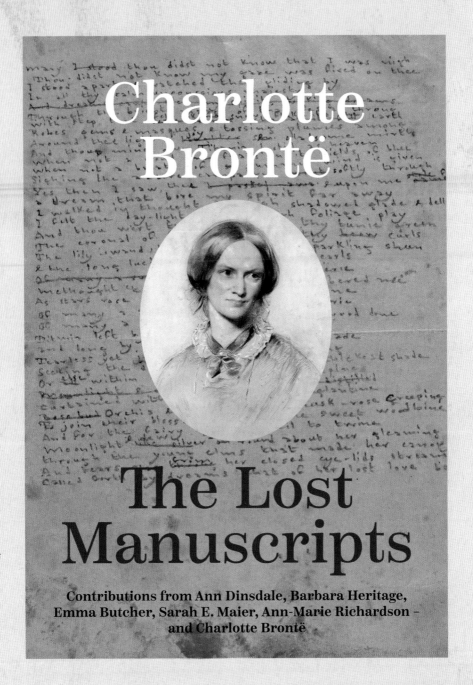

Charlotte Brontë

The Lost Manuscripts

**Contributions from Ann Dinsdale, Barbara Heritage,
Emma Butcher, Sarah E. Maier, Ann-Marie Richardson –
and Charlotte Brontë**

The Brontë Society

First published in the United Kingdom in 2018 by

The Brontë Society
Brontë Parsonage Museum
Church Street, Haworth, Keighley
West Yorkshire, BD22 8DR, United Kingdom

Cover: Charlotte Brontë by George Richmond
© National Portrait Gallery, London

All other photographs © The Brontë Society unless otherwise credited
in the captions

British Library Cataloguing in Publication Data.

A CIP catalogue record for this book is available from the British Library.

ISBN: 978-1-903007-20-4

Designed by Stubbs Design, Ilkley
Editing and production through Westline Publishing Limited, BA12 6NZ
Printed in Europe by Printworks Global Ltd

Contents

Foreword

The Brontë story is an extraordinary one, as is the story of Mrs Brontë's book – and the new manuscripts contained within. When I accepted the role of Brontë Society President at the beginning of the bicentenary celebrations in 2016, I did so with a desire to celebrate and promote the legacy of this fascinating and iconic family during this exciting period. I didn't imagine that there might be a new discovery to celebrate, a precious relic to dwell upon, and yet here we are.

The story of a book "saved from the waves" is a romantic tale, the kind of tale one might find in the Brontë juvenilia, but the significance of Mrs Brontë's book, a two-volume copy of *The Remains of Henry Kirke White*, edited by Robert Southey, and published in 1810, has resonance beyond the mere fact of ownership. Mrs Brontë is an absent presence in the Brontë story. It is unsurprising that the novels of Charlotte, Emily and Anne feature motherless children – their early childhood was indelibly marked by the premature death of their mother at the age of thirty-eight. One cannot help but be moved by the story of Mrs Brontë's book being passed down to her young children, who saw fit to read and re-read, and, I like to imagine, were inspired to write themselves.

It is difficult to convey how special this book is – it is an object imbued with loss but invaluably marked with the presence of the Brontë children. It is also an object that has yielded surprises – a new juvenilia story and poem by Charlotte were discovered slipped inside the book – much to the delight of Brontë scholars.

As a life-long fan of the Brontës, it has been a privilege to learn more about the history of Mrs Brontë's book and read the varied critical responses collected here. My hope is that now this remarkable object has made its way back home to Haworth, it will inspire a new generation of Brontë scholars to reflect, analyse, and critique, and in doing so, reveal more about the life and work of this extraordinary family.

Dame Judi Dench, President of the Brontë Society.

Introduction

Discovering unpublished manuscripts by Charlotte Brontë, one of Britain's greatest and best-loved writers, is a landmark event – and the story behind the find is equally remarkable.

The handwritten fragments, one a short story, the other a poem, first came to light in 2015, more than 150 years after Charlotte's death. Intriguingly, they were discovered within the leaves of a book once belonging to her mother, Maria.

The book, *The Remains of Henry Kirke White*, was one of Maria's personal treasures, and when the ship carrying her possessions was wrecked, the book was "saved from the waves". Following Maria's untimely death the book became a highly valued memento, read by all the Brontë family. It was also used as a repository, with the children and their father adding comments, sketches, doodles and annotations to its pages.

When were Charlotte's manuscripts placed inside the book? Who was responsible for carefully taping them inside? Was it Charlotte's father, Patrick, who outlived all his six children? Was it Charlotte's grieving husband, Arthur Bell Nicholls, or was it the subsequent work of a private collector? We will never know for certain but, with meticulous research, we are beginning to unravel the mystery.

Following Patrick's death in 1861, the household possessions were sold at auction, including Mrs Brontë's copy of *The Remains of Henry Kirke White*. It passed into the hands of private collectors in the United States, and no more was heard of the volume until 2015 when it reached the hands of Randall House, a Californian dealer in rare books. They were instructed to sell the book by its owner, who was aware of its valuable contents.

Randall House contacted the Brontë Parsonage Museum and sent photos of sections of the manuscripts – just enough for the handwriting to be authenticated, but without giving away too much

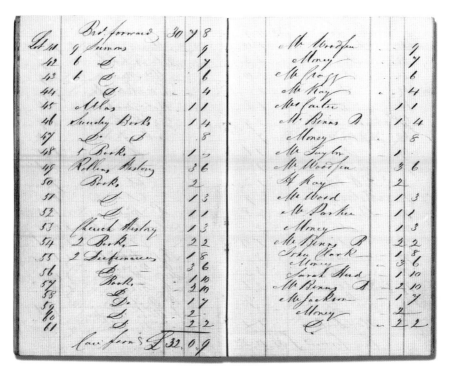

Extract from the handwritten record of the sale of items from the Parsonage following Patrick's death in 1861.

of the exciting content. The book and manuscripts were clearly one of the most important pieces of Brontëana to come to light in decades, and so a major fundraising campaign was launched by the Brontë Society.

Here we acknowledge our debt to the anonymous seller. If the book had gone to auction, there is little doubt that it would have been bought by another private collector.

But instead the Brontë Parsonage Museum was given time to raise the substantial asking price, which they succeeded in doing thanks to a very generous grant from the National Heritage Memorial Fund, and with additional funding from the V&A Purchase Grant Fund and the Friends of the National Libraries. So, finally, in 2016 *The Remains of Henry Kirke White* returned to the Brontë Parsonage Museum in Haworth after an interval of 154 years.

Much has been written about the Brontës, but there are still gaps in our knowledge, and the return of any Brontë relic or manuscript to Haworth provides a rich opportunity to learn more about the family and their work. Mrs Brontë's book was clearly well used and of great sentimental value to the Brontë children who lost their mother while they were still very young. In addition, the unpublished writings by Charlotte offer new opportunities for research.

Now, for the first time, four leading Brontë scholars offer their own interpretations and analysis of this hugely significant find.

Barbara Heritage sets the scene in her essay, *The Archaeology of the Book*, embarking on something akin to an archaeological dig, as, detective-like, she sets about uncovering the story of the book and what it meant to the Brontës. Drawing on all available evidence, she looks at the book through the Brontës' eyes and debates who may have contributed the sketches, doodles and annotations, and why Charlotte's manuscripts, written when she was seventeen years old, were hidden in the book. She reveals the story of Henry Kirke White, and debates whether his writings and premature death relate in any way to the subjects of Charlotte's manuscripts. The many layers of evidence in Mrs Brontë's book are unpicked and revealed in meticulous detail, providing fresh insight into the journey of this precious relic.

Two of the essays focus on the surprise yielded by Mrs Brontë's book – the prose fragment and poem written by Charlotte in her adolescence. In her essay *A Visit To Haworth*, Dr Emma Butcher takes a detailed look at the handwritten prose fragment, unique in all Charlotte's writings. Here, for the first time, Charlotte allows the imaginary world of Glass Town, the subject of her extensive juvenile writings, to merge with her home town, Haworth.

In a story described as "exciting, bawdy, and daring", Charlotte takes her fictionalised hero, Lord Charles Wellesley on a visit to Haworth and allows him to engage (rather offensively!) with the local community. The short story features a public flogging, embezzlement from the Wesleyan chapel, and a caricature of the Reverend John Winterbottom, a religious opponent of Charlotte's father.

In *Fragments of Glass*, Dr Sarah E. Maier looks at both the prose fragment and the poem – which features Mary Percy, a leading character in the Glass Town sagas – found in Mrs Brontë's book. She examines the collaboration between Charlotte and her brother, Branwell, and analyses the role of gender in Charlotte's writing.

Mrs Brontë's copy of *The Remains of Henry Kirke White* would have been read and studied by all the family and in her essay *Reinventing Heaven*, Ann-Marie Richardson focuses on the impact the book may have had on Emily, the most mysterious of the Brontë sisters. She looks at the effect of the book on the structure and psyche of Emily's masterpiece, *Wuthering Heights*, and tantalisingly claims that it is Maria Brontë who haunts its pages.

These four essays offer fresh insight into the intriguing story of the Brontës and are a wonderful addition to Brontë scholarship. Each contributor speaks in their own style and with their own voice, and so, understandably, there are differences in interpretation, and conflicting theories regarding which members of the family may have added their own notes, sketches and doodles.

This is all part of the mystery and will be the subject of debate for many years to come. This remarkable discovery has fired everyone's imagination, and gives 21st century readers a unique glimpse into the world of the Brontës.

LOST AND FOUND

Ann Dinsdale

The story of Maria Brontë's lost book and
the discovery of Charlotte's manuscripts

This is the remarkable story of the discovery of unseen manuscripts, written by Charlotte Brontë when she was just seventeen. They were found in a copy of *The Remains of Henry Kirke White*, edited by Robert Southey, a treasured possession of the Brontë family, and a precious memento of Charlotte's mother, Maria.

Defying all the odds, the book was saved from a shipwreck, sold to a private collector in America – and has finally made its way back to its true home, the Brontë Parsonage Museum in Yorkshire.

Ann Dinsdale is Principal Curator at the Brontë Parsonage Museum in Haworth, where her work involves organising exhibitions and caring for the collection. She is a contributor to *The Brontës in Context* and *A Companion to the Brontës* and author of *At Home with the Brontës: The History of Haworth Parsonage and its Occupants*.

In the autumn of 1812, a ship was driven ashore on the Devonshire coast. No lives were lost in the near-catastrophe, but a great deal of property was never recovered. Amongst the items lost at sea was a trunk containing the possessions of a twenty-nine-year-old Cornish woman, Maria Branwell.

Maria Branwell had left her comfortable home in Penzance earlier in the year to live with relatives in the West Riding of Yorkshire. Once there, she met her uncle's friend and fellow-clergyman, the Reverend Patrick Brontë. Following a whirlwind courtship, the couple became engaged. In a letter written to Patrick shortly before their marriage, Maria informed him:

> *I suppose you never expected to be much the richer for me but I am sorry to inform you that I am still poorer than I thought myself. I mentioned having sent for my books clothes &c On Saturday evg about the time when you were writing the description of your imaginary shipwreck, I was reading & feeling the effects of a real one, having then received a letter from my sister giving me an account of the vessel in which she had sent my box, being stranded on the coast of Devonshire, in consequence of which the box was dashed to pieces with the violence of the sea & all my little property, with the exception of a very few articles swallowed up in the mighty deep.*

One of the items salvaged from the ship was Maria's two-volume copy of *The Remains of Henry Kirke White*, edited by Robert Southey, and published in 1810.

Following Maria's marriage to Patrick Brontë, the book accompanied her to Lousy Thorn Farm at Hartshead, where the couple are believed to have begun their married life, and then to Clough House at Hightown, where their two eldest children, Maria and Elizabeth were born. In 1815 the Brontë family moved to the parsonage at Thornton, near Bradford, where Maria gave birth to the four famous Brontë children: Charlotte (1816), Branwell (1817),

Haworth Parsonage: this is the earliest known photograph of the Parsonage, taken around 1850.

Emily (1818) and Anne (1820). The five years spent at Thornton were pleasant and sociable, but everything changed in 1820 when, shortly after Anne's birth, the family made their final move to Haworth.

Haworth Parsonage, on the edge of the windswept Yorkshire moors, became home to the Brontë family for the rest of their lives. Shortly after the move, Maria became ill with what is believed to have been uterine cancer. She died on September 15th 1821, aged 38, with her husband and sister at her bedside, and her six children huddled at the foot of the bed. The eldest, Maria, was only seven years of age and the youngest, Anne, not yet two. Following her death Mr Brontë added Latin inscriptions to Maria's copy of *The Remains*, recording the fact that the volumes had belonged to his dear wife, that they were "saved from the waves", and should be preserved forever.

Elizabeth Branwell, who had travelled to Yorkshire to help nurse her sister, resigned herself to remaining at Haworth, taking on the role of Parsonage housekeeper and bringing up her nephew and nieces. She took possession of the room that had been her sister's and set about instructing her young nieces in the arts of needlework and household management.

It was always clear that the Brontë children would one day have to be able to support themselves and for the girls, the only acceptable career option open to them was teaching. For this they would need an education beyond that which their aunt could offer, and when a new school for the daughters of impoverished clergymen opened at Cowan Bridge – within a day's travelling distance of Haworth – it must have seemed like an ideal solution. The cost of board and education was subsidised by a reassuringly respectable list of patrons.

In 1824 the four eldest Brontë girls were dispatched to the school. Conditions there were harsh and later provided Charlotte with a model for the infamous Lowood School in her novel *Jane Eyre*. The following year both Maria and Elizabeth were sent home in ill-health and died at the Parsonage within a few weeks of each other, aged eleven and ten years.

For the next few years the four surviving children remained at the Parsonage, receiving lessons from their father and reading any

COWAN BRIDGE SCHOOL, 1824.

Cowan Bridge School, the model for Lowood School in *Jane Eyre*.

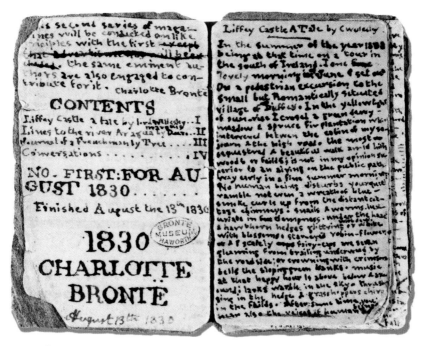

One of the famous 'little books' produced by the Brontës in childhood.

books they could lay their hands on. *The Remains of Henry Kirke White* might be a precious memento of their mother, but it was also well-read and annotated by different members of the family. As with all the Parsonage books, it provided source material for their rich creative lives.

The Brontë children immersed themselves in an imaginary world, sparked by their father's gift to Branwell of a set of toy soldiers. They began to produce their own tiny illustrated books, designed to be small enough for the toy soldiers to "read" (but not the Parsonage adults) and intended to look as though they had been printed. Over the years the siblings paired off, with Charlotte and Branwell developing the imaginary kingdom of Angria, while Emily and Anne created Gondal, an island in the North Pacific. Documenting the goings-on in Angria and Gondal continued to absorb the children into adulthood and, in the case of Charlotte, Emily and Anne, formed the basis of their later literary achievements.

The sisters went on to spend varying lengths of time at Miss Wooler's school at Roe Head, near Mirfield, where Charlotte met her lifelong friend, Ellen Nussey. This was followed by brief, unhappy periods working away from home as governesses. In 1842 Charlotte and Emily travelled to Brussels to brush up on their language skills, in preparation for opening a school of their own. The study trip was funded by their Aunt (Elizabeth) Branwell, and it was news of her illness which brought them back to Haworth in less than a year. Their aunt died before they reached home and while Emily remained at the Parsonage as housekeeper, Charlotte returned to Brussels. She finally came home in 1844, suffering the pains of unrequited love for her teacher, Monsieur Heger. The school project foundered when no pupils could be found.

While Emily thrived in the safe environment of the Parsonage, her siblings struggled to make their way in the world. This was particularly the case with their brother, Branwell, who was left floundering after several attempts to earn his living had all ended ignominiously. Although he still hoped to establish himself as a published author, it was beginning to look increasingly unlikely ever to happen.

The sisters had continued to write and in 1846, they used part of a legacy from Aunt Branwell to finance the publication of their poems, concealing their true identities under the pseudonyms of Currer, Ellis and Acton Bell. When only two copies of their *Poems* were sold, each sister set to work writing a novel. Charlotte's first attempt at writing a novel for publication was *The Professor*, which was rejected by several publishers, eventually appearing posthumously in 1857. She experienced more success with her second attempt, *Jane Eyre*, which was published to instant acclaim in October 1847. Two months later Emily's *Wuthering Heights* and Anne's *Agnes Grey* were

Left: The three sisters, Anne, Emily and Charlotte, painted by their brother, Branwell c. 1834.

© National Portrait Gallery, London

The dining room at the Brontë Parsonage Museum. This is where the Brontë sisters worked, and where they took it in turns to read aloud to each other as they walked around the table.

published by Thomas Cautley Newby. Anne's second novel, *The Tenant of Wildfell Hall*, followed in June 1848.

Later that year, tragedy struck. Branwell died on September 24th after months spent in an alcohol-fuelled decline. Emily's death from consumption followed on December 19th and Anne succumbed to the same disease on May 28th 1849. Charlotte published two more novels – *Shirley* (1849) and *Villette* (1853).

Patrick Brontë stayed on at the Parsonage after the death of all six of his children.

Her fame provided her with a means of entering London's literary society, but bereavement and the seclusion of her life at Haworth left her unfit to enjoy the rewards of her celebrity. In 1854 she married her father's curate, Arthur Bell Nicholls, but died in the early stages of pregnancy on March 31st 1855.

Patrick Brontë outlived his wife and all of his children. He died in June 1861 and, in October of that year, the Brontës' books – along with all their household goods – were sold at auction. The sale had not been widely advertised and was attended mainly by local people. The titles and whereabouts of many of the books sold over the two days of the sale remain unknown. The handwritten sale catalogue, held at the Brontë Parsonage Museum, lists various lots consisting of 'Sundry Books' and 'Books', including Lot 51, an anonymous assortment of books which was knocked down to the Reverend J. H. Wood, the Baptist minister at Haworth, for the sum of 1s 3d. We now know that the Brontës' copy of *The Remains of Henry Kirke White* formed part of this lot.

By the end of the decade the book had travelled with a new owner to America. It was rebound to form a single volume and a collection of letters recording its provenance were inserted inside. These serve to document the various hands through which it subsequently passed.

The book came to light again in 2015 after it had been placed with a dealer in rare books based in California. By this time its value – in both financial and research terms – had been greatly enhanced by the addition of two previously unknown original manuscripts by Charlotte Brontë, which had been tipped inside the book. These offer intriguing insights into Charlotte's wit and powers of observation, as well as her gift for imagery. They also offer an important new resource for furthering research into the Brontës' lives and works.

The book has made what is likely to be its final journey, returning to Haworth after being purchased by the Brontë Parsonage Museum. The huge significance of the book and its contents was reflected in the generous level of support its acquisition attracted from the National Heritage Memorial Fund (NHMF), the V&A Purchase Grant Fund and the Friends of the National Libraries (FNL).

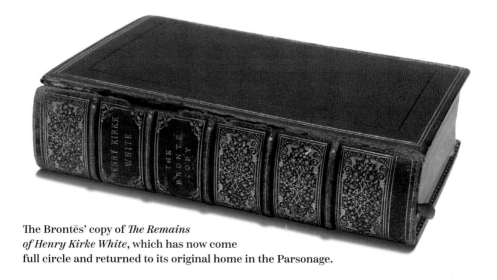

The Brontës' copy of *The Remains of Henry Kirke White*, which has now come full circle and returned to its original home in the Parsonage.

THE ARCHAEOLOGY OF THE BOOK

Barbara Heritage

And hee said unto mee, Sonne of man, can these bones live? and I answered, O Lord God, thou knowest.

Ezekiel 37:3, King James Bible

So many books have witnessed and endured extraordinary events as part of their lives in private collections, but usually, over time, those histories are eventually lost, effaced, overlooked, or forgotten. This essay traces the historical provenance of a remarkable copy of the fourth edition of *The Remains of Henry Kirke White* – a book that was first owned and read by Maria Brontë in Penzance, then nearly lost at sea before travelling to Yorkshire, where it was voraciously read and carefully preserved by the Brontë family.

Over time, the *Remains* was treated as both a memorial and memento, becoming an object of bibliophilic study and fascination, while serving as the receptacle for two formerly unknown fragments of Charlotte's juvenilia. Studying the *Remains*, layer by layer, the history of this unique artefact is recovered, including its journeys in England and abroad, and revealing the many lives it touched.

Barbara Heritage is Associate Director and Curator of Collections of the Rare Book School at the University of Virginia. She is currently completing a book titled *Charlotte Brontë and the Labor of Writing*. She serves on the Council of the Bibliographical Society of America, and is a member of the Grolier Club, the oldest existing bibliophilic club in North America.

Timeline

1803: Henry Kirke White's *Clifton Grove* is published.

1804: Robert Southey corresponds with White; Charles Simeon procures a sizarship for White to attend St. John's College, Cambridge; White takes a year to prepare for university, and undertakes intensive studies with a tutor; White becomes ill.

1805: White enters St. John's College and distinguishes himself; Patrick Brontë advises White regarding living expenses.

1806: Henry Kirke White dies in his rooms at Cambridge in October; Robert Southey receives White's papers in December, and begins editing them.

1807: The first edition of the *Remains* is published.

1808: The second and third editions of the *Remains* are published.

1810: The fourth edition of the *Remains* is published and is obtained, shortly thereafter, by Maria Branwell in Penzance.

1812: Maria Branwell moves to the West Riding of Yorkshire, where she meets Patrick Brontë; the two are engaged to marry; Maria sends for her belongings in Penzance – a delivery that is delayed when the ship *Trader* is driven ashore on October 23 at Ilfracombe, Devon; Maria and Patrick are married in December.

1813-1820: Maria Brontë gives birth to Maria, Elizabeth, Charlotte, Branwell, Emily, and Anne Brontë.

1821: Maria dies in Haworth from uterine cancer, and is survived by Patrick and their six children.

1825: Daughters Maria and Elizabeth return from Cowan Bridge School; both die from tuberculosis.

1829: Earliest recorded manuscript of prose fiction written by Charlotte Brontë.

c. 1833: Charlotte drafts unnamed poetry and prose manuscript fragments, later included in the *Remains*.

1836-37: Charlotte corresponds with Southey.

1841: Branwell writes the poem *Lord Nelson*, after "NELSONI. MORS. H. K. WHITE" as published in the *Remains*.

1847: The first edition of *Jane Eyre* is published; the first editions of *Wuthering Heights* and *Agnes Grey* are published together in three volumes.

1848: Second and third editions of *Jane Eyre* are published; Branwell dies (most likely from tuberculosis and complications from substance abuse), followed by Emily, who also dies from tuberculosis; *The Tenant of Wildfell Hall* is published.

1849: Anne dies from tuberculosis; *Shirley* is published.

1853: *Villette* is published.

1854: Charlotte marries Arthur Bell Nicholls.

1855: Charlotte dies (most likely from complications owing to her pregnancy); Reverend J. H. Wood sends a letter of condolence to Nicholls and receives a reply from Nicholls, later bound into the *Remains*.

1857: The first edition of *The Life of Charlotte Brontë* is published.

1861: Patrick dies in Haworth on June 7; on October 2, the *Remains* is sold at auction with Patrick's household effects and is purchased by Wood, Baptist minister at Haworth.

1861-69: Wood inscribes the *Remains* and gives it to the Reverend Edwin Paxton Hood at an unknown time between 1861 and 1869.

1869: Hood sends the *Remains*, as well as a Bible used by Charlotte and a copy of the *Medulla Historiae Anglicanae* annotated by Jonathan Swift, to the Reverend Thomas Binney for shipment to Reverend William Buell Sprague in the United States.

1869-70: Sprague receives the *Remains*, Charlotte's Bible and the *Medulla Historiae Anglicanae*.

1876: William Buell Sprague dies.

1878: The *Remains* is auctioned off in May in New York City by Bangs & Company as part of the "concluding portion" of the sale of Sprague's vast collection; it is most likely purchased by John A. Spoor.

1878-1915: Judge Joseph F. Daly acquires the *Remains* from Spoor at some point between 1878 and 1915.

1916: Judge Joseph F. Daly dies; the *Remains* is auctioned off in New York City by Anderson Galleries as part of the Daly sale, and is purchased by Mary McMillin Norton.

1918: The *Remains* is once again auctioned off in New York City by Anderson Galleries as part of the Mary McMillin Norton sale; the *Remains* is purchased by a family who hold it in their collection until 2015.

2016: The Brontë Parsonage Museum acquires the *Remains*.

We are accustomed to reading books for the printed works they contain, written by authors both living and dead – and sometimes long dead. Like that "grey marble tablet" described in *Jane Eyre* as marking the grave of Helen Burns and bearing the engraved word "Resurgam", books afford writers the chance to rise again and speak to new generations of readers. Books are survivors, in some cases, of wars, shipwrecks, fires, and floods. They cannot be made to vanish at the push of a button. Their intractable physical presence is part of their power. Even as we each shuffle off our own mortal coil, books survive, their bindings, paper, type, and illustrations remain intact, thus preserving and carrying with them not only the words of their authors, but also the material histories of former times.

Indeed, physical books are one of our most important links to the past. After coins, books are perhaps the most prevalent of surviving historical artefacts. Yet unlike coins, physical books serve as both tablets and containers, carrying with them not only the words of their authors and the evidence of their manufacture, but also the various marks of use made by former readers and owners: inscriptions, erasures, marginalia, doodles, pinpricks, dog-eared leaves, and external additions such as bookmarks, photographs, or pressed plants; they may also have omissions, such as missing leaves or plates. These physical traces survive for future readers to find, creating additional tangible links with the past.

In this way, books are like archaeological sites: the alterations made by various hands are like the layering of deposits – the strata developing yet another layer of historical residue with the activities of present-day readers and owners. Books are not only *about* history: they constitute and embody the living historical record itself. It is precisely because books have this power to encapsulate the past that they serve as reminders of the tenuousness of the present. Every "old book" is a *memento mori*, outliving former owners and reminding us that we are only temporary curators of the history we hold in our hands.

The Brontë children made sketches in their copy of Goldsmith's *Grammar of General Geography*.

The Brontë family were sensitive to such historical resonances. They owned, read, and annotated a number of used and antiquarian volumes, primarily owing to the circumstance that Patrick Brontë's modest income of £170 a year[1] as Perpetual Curate and officiating minister at the church of St. Michael's and All Angels in Haworth allowed him little extra money for purchasing new books. Second- or third-hand books, generally sold at reduced prices, were more affordable for a man in Patrick's position. At the same time, the histories of those antique volumes were palpable to the Brontë children, as we see in the following diary entry made by Charlotte in March of 1829:

> *Once papa lent my Sister Mar[ia] A Book it was an old Geography and she wrote on its Blank leaf papa lent me this Book. The Book is an hundred and twen[ty] years old it is at this moment lying Before me while I write this.*[2]

1   Juliet Barker, *The Brontës* (London: Weidenfeld and Nicolson, 1994), p. 105.
2   MS Bonnell80(11), Brontë Parsonage Museum, Haworth, England.

Charlotte was only twelve years old when she made this observation, copying out her oldest sister's annotation. Maria had died from pulmonary tuberculosis just four years earlier, at the age of eleven. Although Maria was dead, her handwriting survived for Charlotte to discover. The antiquarian book in question thus contained more than a lesson in geography – it also contained a remnant of Maria herself. Maria would eventually return in the form of yet another book – one authored by Charlotte. For it was Maria who would serve as the model for Helen Burns in *Jane Eyre*.

Like the ouroboros – the serpent consuming its own tail – we come full circle: to a particular copy of *The Remains of Henry Kirke White*, published in 1810, and brought into the family by Maria Brontë, Patrick Brontë's wife and the mother of his children. This book, which was published to memorialise the premature death of a young English poet, would not only survive near destruction by being rescued from a stranded ship; it would also serve as a kind of reliquary for the writings of the Brontë family. Urn-like, it would come to contain inscriptions by Patrick Brontë, marginalia by the Brontë children, inserted leaves containing manuscript juvenilia by Charlotte, a letter on mourning stationery by Charlotte's widower, Arthur Bell Nicholls, as well as numerous notes and materials inserted by later book collectors who obtained the volume.

An artefact as complex as the Brontës' copy of the *Remains* requires close interpretation and physical analysis. Who was it that first placed Charlotte's manuscript fragments and Arthur Bell Nicholls' letter into the *Remains*? Were the manuscripts saved by Patrick Brontë, or were they acquired by a collector who later added them to the book? Why were the *Remains* chosen as the receptacle for Charlotte's fragments? Did the book's subject – the writings and premature death of Henry Kirke White – relate in any way to the subjects of Charlotte's manuscripts? How did this book come to attract so many collectors, who themselves sought to alter it and expand upon its history?

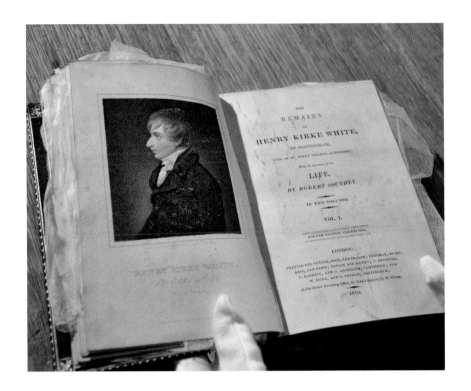

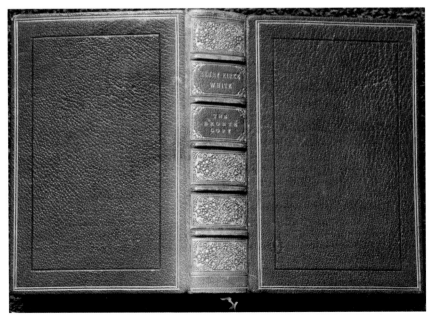

The Brontë family's copy of *The Remains of Henry Kirke White*.

Today, if you visit the Brontë Parsonage Museum at Haworth, you will find that the museum's copy of *The Remains of Henry Kirke White, of Nottingham, Late of St. John's College, Cambridge; with an Account of His Life* is replete with inserted manuscript materials, as well as notes, marginalia, annotations, and clippings that have been added to the book over the course of two hundred years. The book is bound in pebble-grained goatskin (frequently, if inexactly, described in dealer descriptions as "Levant morocco") of a rich caramel colour. The book's front and back covers are identically decorated with a simple rectangular border, hand-tooled in blind (i.e., without gold) within a double rectangular border of parallel lines tooled in gold. The spine, richly and intricately tooled in gold with stars, arabesques, and other designs, is similarly lettered in gold:

HENRY KIRKE / WHITE / THE / BRONTÉ / COPY

The book is clearly a collector's copy – a trophy, of sorts – intended for conspicuous display.

But to start at the beginning, we have to picture the *Remains* as Maria Branwell first read it in 1810, before her marriage to Patrick and before the birth of her remarkable children. The book, in two illustrated, octavo volumes, was handsomely printed on watermarked, wove paper. A contemporary advertisement for the book ran as follows:

> *This day is published, a new Edition, in two vols, 8vo, with an elegant Head of the Author, and other plates, price 14s. boards.*
>
> *THE REMAINS of HENRY KIRKE WHITE, of Nottingham, late of St. John's College, Cambridge; with an account of his Life, by ROBT. SOUTHEY.*
>
> *Printed for Vernor, Good, and Sharpe; Longman, Hurst, Rees, and Orme, London; J. Deighton, T. Barrett, and J. Nicholson, Cambridge; and sold by Stevenson, Matchett, and Stevenson, and all other booksellers in Norwich and Norfolk.*[3]

3   *The Norfolk Chronicle and Norwich Gazette* (Norwich, England), Saturday, February 17, 1810; p. 1; issue 2082.

In 1810, the *Remains* sold for 14 shillings – a real price cost equivalent to about £45 in 2018 currency.[4] Maria was raised in a prosperous, middle-class family, residing in Penzance, Cornwall, who could readily afford such goods. Maria's father had died in 1808, leaving her a life annuity of £50 per annum.[5] When originally sold, the two volumes would probably have had more or less temporary covers consisting of paper spines with printed labels, and paper sides covering thin cardboard, a typical binding at the time for new books of this sort. Once having purchased such a book, owners might have it rebound more permanently, usually in sheep, calf, or goat, for an additional fee. But it is quite possible, for reasons that will be stated later, that Maria kept her copy of the *Remains* as it was first sold: in its original paper-covered boards.

By 1810, *The Remains of Henry Kirke White* was already in its fourth edition. The book was initially published in 1807 – just one year after White's untimely death from tuberculosis at the age of 21 – by a group of enterprising publishers and booksellers. The firm of Vernor, Hood, and Sharpe was located in London; their speciality was publishing affordable texts containing illustrations, such as prints and maps. They were responsible for the book's attractive engraved half title and illustrations, which included a stipple portrait frontispiece of White, aged 21 years, by Samuel Freeman and based on a painting made by Thomas Barber of Nottingham. Some years before the publication of the *Remains*, Vernor and Hood had published White's early writings in *The Monthly Mirror*, as well as his first and only book, *Clifton Grove, A Sketch in Verse, with Other Poems* (1803), whose text was included in the *Remains*.

The publishing combine responsible for the 1807 edition included the London firm of Longman, Hurst, Rees, and Orme, a long-established firm well-known for having published the works of several leading Romantic poets, including Robert Southey (who,

4   Lawrence H. Officer and Samuel H. Williamson, "Five Ways to Compute the Relative Value of a UK Pound Amount, 1270 to Present," MeasuringWorth, 2018.

5   Juliet Barker, *The Brontës* (London: Weidenfeld and Nicolson, 1994), pp. 50-51.

with the aid of White's family, supplied a biographical account of White for the publication), as well as William Wordsworth, Samuel Taylor Coleridge, and Sir Walter Scott. In addition, the project was financed by the Cambridge booksellers J. Dighton, T. Barrett, and J. Nicholson, logical choices, given White's studies and connections at St. John's College. It was distributed by the printer-booksellers W. Dunn and S. Tupman, located in Nottingham, Henry Kirke White's hometown. By 1810, the London publishing firm of Taylor and Hessey had joined the enterprise, too.

Robert Southey's involvement was key to the publication of the *Remains*. Although White's early writings had attracted some favourable notice, his book *Clifton Grove* had received a negative review in *The Monthly Review* shortly after its initial publication in 1803. In an unsigned review, the dissenting minister and journalist, Christopher Lake Moody, had critiqued White's work as follows:

> As a book which is to 'win its way' on the sole ground of its own merit, this poem cannot be contemplated with any sanguine expectation … we commend his exertions and his laudable endeavours to excel: but we cannot compliment him with having already learned the difficult art of writing good poetry.[6]

Deeply discouraged by this criticism, White submitted a letter of complaint to the editor of *The Monthly Review*, who upheld Moody's anonymous opinion. Indeed, the journal maintained its position even after the *Remains* was published and generally acclaimed.

Upon reading this negative review, Southey wrote to White to encourage and advise him. The two briefly corresponded before falling out of contact once Southey learned that White was being aided by the influential Evangelical minister, Charles Simeon. As Southey wrote to a friend, "I plainly saw that the Evangelicals had caught him."[7] Simeon had decided to sponsor White, allowing him

6   Christopher Lake Moody, "Review of Clifton Grove," *The Monthly Review* 43 (February 1804): p. 218.

7   *The Life and Correspondence of the Late Robert Southey*, ed. Rev. Charles Cuthbert Southey, vol. 3 of 6 (London: Longman, Brown, Green, and Longmans, 1850), p. 92.

The poet, Henry Kirke White, was just 21 when he died.

to obtain a sizarship to attend St. John's College, Cambridge. At
university, the ambitious White, who had suffered from poor health
in the past, was greatly taxed by overwork and ill health. He died at
Cambridge from tuberculosis shortly after beginning his studies there.

Southey received a notice from White's family informing him
of the poet's death, to which he replied, inquiring whether the family
intended to publish any of White's remaining works, and whether
they would like his assistance in doing so. The family replied,

entrusting Southey with an extraordinary package containing numerous poems, letters, fragments, prose compositions, and reflections, some containing references to Calvinist and Methodist practices, most of them informed by White's fervent Evangelicalism. As Southey recollected to a friend:

Down came a box-full, the sight of which literally made my heart ache, and my eyes overflow, for never did I behold such proofs of human industry. To make short, I took the matter up with interest, collected his letters, and have, at the expense of more time than such a poor fellow as myself can very well afford, done what his family are very grateful for, and what I think the world will thank me for too. […] Among his letters there is a great deal of Methodism: if this procures for the book, as it very likely may, a sale among the righteous over-much, I shall rejoice for the sake of his family, for whom I am very much interested.[8]

Southey edited the papers without payment, and prepared an account of White's life to accompany them.

Southey also provided an additional account of receiving the papers in the *Remains*, recalling how:

Mr. Coleridge was present when I opened them, and was, as well as myself, equally affected and astonished at the proofs of industry which they displayed ... His poems were numerous: among the earliest, was a sonnet addressed to myself, long before the little intercourse which had subsisted between us had taken place. Little did he think, when it was written, on what occasion it would fall into my hands.[9]

These tragic circumstances – as well as the belated recovery of White's poetry by Southey – would only enhance the popularity of the *Remains*.

8 *The Life and Correspondence of the Late Robert Southey*, ed. Rev. Charles Cuthbert Southey, vol. 3 of 6 (London: Longman, Brown, Green, and Longmans, 1850), pp. 92-93.

9 *Remains*, fourth edition, pp. 52-53.

Robert Southey was a successful poet in his own right, and was determined that Kirke White's work should be commemorated.

Portrait of Southey by Robert Hancock, black, red and brown chalk and pencil, 1796.

© National Portrait Gallery, London

In 1813, Southey would be named Poet Laureate. When the *Remains* was initially published in 1807, however, Southey was already a highly regarded poet, as well as a well-known literary critic, historian, journalist, editor, and translator. In 1803, he and Joseph Cottle had edited a collected edition of poetry by Thomas Chatterton, a precocious writer who had committed suicide at the age of 17, and who was subsequently commemorated in poems by John Keats, Percy Bysshe Shelley, William Wordsworth, and Samuel Taylor Coleridge. In the *Remains*, Southey drew a direct parallel between the two young men, asserting:

> *I have inspected all the existing manuscripts of Chatterton, and they excited less wonder than these … Much has been suppressed, which, if Henry had been, like Chatterton, of another generation, I should willingly have published, and the world would willingly have received; but in doing honor to the dead, I have been scrupulously careful never to forget the living.*[10]

Indeed, White was likely to have been familiar with Southey's own edition of Chatterton's works; earlier on, at the age of 15, White had lectured on Chatterton's genius at the Nottingham Literary Society.[11] In a letter to White's brother, Southey made his own editorial ambitions clear. Speaking of other young men who had the same "uphill path to tread," Southey wrote that "[Henry] will be to them what Chatterton was to him, and he will be a purer and better example."[12]

White's poetry and writings – carefully presented by Southey within the context of White's ambitious struggle for literary success, his pious life, and premature death – elicited a satisfying pathos for early nineteenth century readers. As one reviewer of the *Remains* noted, the melancholy cast of White's poetry conveyed an "awful pleasure,"[13] such as that elicited by the following passage in which White envisions his own death in Wilford Churchyard:

> *I would not have my corpse cemented down*
> *With brick and stone, defrauding the poor earth-worm*

---

10 *Remains*, fourth edition, p. 54.

11 Terry Fry, "Henry Kirke White: Poet and Hymn Writer, 1785-1806." *Articles from the Thoroton Society Newsletter*, accessed 11 January 2018: http://www.thorotonsociety.org.uk/publications/articles/kirkewhite.htm. Southey describes the lecture on pages 11 and 12 of the 1810 edition, but does not mention Chatterton's name.

12 *The Life and Correspondence of the Late Robert Southey*, ed. Rev. Charles Cuthbert Southey, vol. 3 of 6 (London: Longman, Brown, Green, and Longmans, 1850), p. 61.

13 *The Monthly Mirror* (March 1809), pp. 149-155.

Of its predestined dues; no, I would lie
Beneath a little hillock, grass o'ergrown,
Swath'd down with oziers, just as sleep the cotters.
Yet may not undistinguish'd be my grave;
But there at eve may some congenial soul,
Duly resort, and shed a pious tear,
The good man's benzoin—no more I ask.

The fact that the same poem bore the following epigraph, *On Recovery from Sickness*, only heightened the prophetic quality of White's writings, and, in light of his death, encouraged readers to read White's works as autobiography.

White's poems were certainly proleptic, if not prescient, even as his very life and death followed a familiar Chatterton-like pattern. As another reviewer of the *Remains* remarked:

> *In the Temple of Fame, as in the Elysium of Virgil, a peculiar region ought to be consecrated to the victims of a premature destiny.*

White was a type – one of those "*infantum animæ* […] snatched from the world *in limine primo*."[14]

The same reviewer noted:

> …*church-yard scenes and cypress groves at the dreadful noon of night, silence, darkness, solitude, contemplation, and egotism, with overpowering melancholy, and fast-approaching death,— such is the funereal train that walks in sad procession round the sleepless pillow of the sentimental bard.*[15]

Had life and art not so closely intermixed, heightening the flavour of White's poems, his writings (the same reviewer hinted) might not have been so well remembered.

There was yet another vital component of the *Remains* that justified its many editions and growing popularity among readers:

14 *The Monthly Review, or Literary Journal, Enlarged* 61 (January 1810): p. 71.
15 *The Monthly Review*, p. 73.

an ever-increasing collection of "tributary verses" supplied by an expanding list of admirers appeared in subsequent editions of the *Remains* along with Southey's biographical sketch and White's poems. The steel-engraved half title – which featured a flaming urn bearing the legend *HIS MONUMENT SHALL BE HIS NAME ALONE* enhanced the sense that the book was a living tribute, as did the additional quotation taken from Byron's *Epitaph on a Friend* engraved in fair letters beneath the entire vignette:

> *No marble marks thy couch of lowly sleep / But living statues, there are seen to weep: Affliction's semblance bends not o-er thy tomb, / Affliction's self deplores thy youthful doom.*

It was this memorial-like quality of the *Remains* that made the book a living publication: for each of the early editions featured new literary offerings by additional contributors. The first edition of 1807 included ten tributary verses written by friends and acquaintances, including the Cambridge-educated lawyer and minor political figure, Capel Lofft (who appeared as "C. L."), as well as the Reverend James Plumptre, the Rector of Great Gransden, Cambridgeshire. Just two of the tributary poems had been presented to White during his life – chiefly, in defence of his published poems – while the rest were eulogies commemorating his untimely death.

A number of these tributary poems contain short subtitles and epigraphs suggestive of their own provenance. For instance, one poem is titled as follows:

> *WRITTEN IN THE HOMER OF MR. H. KIRKE WHITE. Presented to me by his Brother, J. Neville White.*

Another is titled:

> *STANZAS. Supposed to have been written at the Grave of H. K. White. BY A LADY.*

Such notes emphasised each poem's origin in real artefacts and documents, heightening the sense that the *Remains* served as both an actual collection and urn-like reliquary.

The second edition of the *Remains*, published in 1808, included seven additional tributary poems. Another eulogy was added in the third edition (also published in 1808):

To the Memory of Henry Kirke White, by the Reverend W. B. Collyer.

And yet seven more elegiac verses were added in the 1810 fourth edition. By then, the tributary poems had led to a multiplier effect – to the extent that the fourth edition's last contributed verse, written by a Mrs M. Hay, explicitly announced that it was written in response to reading the *Remains* itself:

LINES. Written on reading the Remains of Henry Kirke White, of Nottingham, late of St. John's College, Cambridge; with an Account of his Life, by Robert Southey, Esq.

Perhaps, following on the heels of the late eighteenth-century cult of sensibility, it was appropriate for White's own self-reflexive poems to attract sentimental displays of grief. The *Remains* was not only a memorial, but also a kind of mirror, wherein readers could see themselves, and perhaps even place themselves in print. For White's readers, the activities of reading, mourning, and writing were directly interlinked. And, as Southey had predicted, many of White's readers were Methodists, whose sympathies for the poet were heightened by the virtuous nature of his verse.

Very few of the tributary poems contributed by White's mourners and admirers could be considered literary works in themselves. In 1811, Byron would add the most notable offering in the form of an extract taken from his satirical poem, *English Bards and Scotch Reviewers*. In that extract, Byron plays on the association of writing and quill pens. Henry is likened to an eagle struck in the heart by a "fatal dart," but not before realising that the shaft of the dart is adorned with and guided by his very own "feather":

THE
REMAINS

OF

HENRY KIRKE WHITE,

OF NOTTINGHAM,

LATE OF ST. JOHN'S COLLEGE, CAMBRIDGE;

With an Account of his

LIFE,

BY ROBERT SOUTHEY.

IN TWO VOLUMES.

VOL. I.

FOURTH EDITION, CORRECTED.

LONDON:

PRINTED FOR VERNOR, HOOD, AND SHARPE; LONGMAN, HURST,
REES, AND ORME; TAYLOR AND HESSEY; J. DEIGHTON,
T. BARRETT, AND J. NICHOLSON, CAMBRIDGE; AND
W. DUNN, AND S. TUPMAN, NOTTINGHAM;

At the Union Printing-Office, St. John's Square, by W. Wilson.

1810.

Keen were his pangs, but keener far to feel
He nurs'd the pinion which impell'd the steel,
While the same plumage that had warm'd his nest,
Drank the last life-drop of his bleeding breast.[16]

Thus, the poet was killed by his own pen.

MARIA'S PERSONAL COPY

Byron's 1811 contribution aside, such was the book that Maria Branwell acquired around the age of 27. Most likely, she would have been encouraged in such reading.

In 1810, Penzance had its own circulating library, as well as the Penzance Ladies' Book Club, established in 1770 (preceding the Penzance's Gentlemen's Book Club, which was founded shortly afterward).[17] The women in the club read a "carefully selected range" of poetry and novels, as well as histories, biographies, travel narratives, and suchlike.[18] That so many of the tributary poems appearing in the *Remains* were written by "lady" readers suggests that the book would have been popularly read by genteel audiences of women, such as those in Penzance, perhaps especially among women who were Methodists. It was certainly the case that members of the Branwell family were staunch Wesleyan Methodists. (In 1814, the family would supply substantial funds toward the erection of Penzance's first Methodist chapel.[19]) White's evangelically-inspired writing would likely have made it a welcome choice for Maria. As a critic for *The Anti-Jacobin Review* noted

16 *Remains*, fifth edition, vol. 1 of 2, (London: Vernor, Hood, and Sharpe; Longman, Hurst, Rees, Orme, and Brown; and Taylor and Hessey), p. 310.

17 J. S. Courtney, *A Guide to Penzance and Its Neighborhood* (Penzance: E. Rowe; also London: Longman, Brown, Green, and Longman), p. 37.

18 Catherine Ingrassia, ed. *The Cambridge Companion to Women's Writing in Britain, 1660-1789* (Cambridge: Cambridge University Press, 2016), p. 27.

19 *The Oxford Companion to the Brontës*, p. 58.

Left: Title page of the Brontë's own copy of the *Remains*.

Watercolour painting of the house in Penzance where Maria Branwell grew up.

in 1809, the *Remains* described White's "inward conviction of the true religion." Although for some readers, the *Remains* may "appear strongly to savour of what is termed methodism," for others the poems would serve as a "glowing testimony to the triumphant superiority of pure religion."[20]

Maria and her copy of the *Remains* would not long reside in Penzance, however. After the death of her uncle in 1812, Maria

20 *The Anti-Jacobin Review and Magazine or Monthly Political and Literary Censor* 32, no. 130 (April 1809), 352-57: p. 353.

moved away from the town to live in the West Riding of Yorkshire, with her aunt, Jane, wife of the Reverend John Fennell, and to earn her living at Woodhouse Grove, a boarding school for Methodist ministers' sons where Fennell was headmaster.[21] Shortly after her arrival there, Maria met Patrick Brontë. They were soon engaged to be married and, preparing for this, Maria sent for her remaining books and clothes from Penzance.

Packed into a box with Maria's other effects, the *Remains* began its journey up the coast of England in a boat that became – not shipwrecked, as is often recounted – stranded on the coast of Devonshire.[22] The *Remains* is thought to have been transported on the ship, *Trader*, driven ashore on October 23rd at Ilfracombe, Devon, during her voyage from Penzance, Cornwall, to Bristol, Gloucestershire.[23] As Maria later relayed via a letter to Patrick:

> *the box was dashed to pieces with the violence of the sea & all my little property, with the exception of a very few articles, swallowed up in the mighty deep.*[24]

Although the *Remains* does not bear any discernable damage from seawater, Maria's issues of *The Lady's Magazine* were later described by Charlotte as having been "discoloured by brine."[25]

Now safely delivered to Maria, the *Remains* moved with her and Patrick from Hartshead, where Patrick was a curate, to Thornton, and then finally to Haworth. During that time, between 1813 and 1820, Maria gave birth to six children – Maria, Elizabeth, Charlotte, Branwell, Emily and Anne – before dying at Haworth in 1821, most likely from uterine cancer.[26]

---

21 Juliet Barker, *The Brontës* (London: Weidenfeld and Nicolson, 1994), p. 51.

22 In her letter to Patrick, Maria clearly describes "the vessel [...] being stranded on the coast of Devonshire." See Maria Branwell's letter written to Patrick Brontë, 18 Nov 1812; quoted in Barker, p. 55.

23 "Lloyd's Marine List – Oct. 27, 1812." *Caledonian Mercury.* 31 October 1812.

24 See Maria Branwell's letter written to Patrick Brontë, 18 Nov 1812; quoted in Barker, p. 55.

25 Charlotte Brontë, *The Letters of Charlotte Brontë*, ed. Margaret Smith, vol. 1: 1829-1847 (Oxford: Clarendon Press 1995): p. 240.

26 *The Oxford Companion to the Brontës*, p. 63.

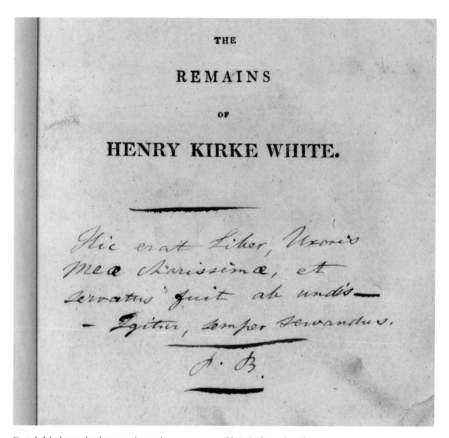

Patrick's inscription, written in memory of his beloved wife.

A FAMILY MEMENTO

One day after Maria's death, Patrick wrote the following inscription
in brown ink on the half-title page of the first volume of the *Remains*:

———

Hic erat Liber, Uxonis
mea charissimæ, et
servatus fuit ab undis—
—Igitur, semper servandus.

———

P.B.

———

Translated from Latin into English, Patrick's inscription reads as follows:

This was the Book, of my most beloved Wife, and it had been saved from the waves—Therefore, it must always be preserved.

The inscription was fitting, serving to commemorate Maria, his wife, even as the *Remains* memorialised White. The choice of Latin further emphasised the enduring, epitaph-like quality of the inscription.

The second volume of the Brontë copy of the *Remains* features a similar inscription in Patrick's hand on its half-title page, but it is also clear that, here, a portion of the inscription has been cut away where the volume was later trimmed while being rebound. This evidence suggests two important points: first, that both Patrick and Maria read the book as two volumes, hence the twin inscriptions, which would not have been necessary had the volumes been bound together into a single volume after their purchase in 1810; second, that Patrick was concerned that the volumes would be unintentionally discarded after his own death. At the time when Patrick owned the volumes, they may have appeared in a somewhat ragged state. Indeed, one source, admittedly not entirely reliable,

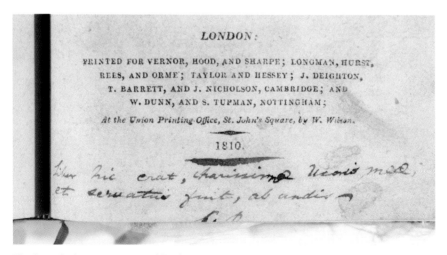

The inscription was repeated in the second volume.

states that the books were "coverless" by the time of Patrick's death.[27] If the volumes had remained in their original bindings of paper-covered boards, they very well might have eventually fallen off owing to heavy use.

Although Patrick sedulously preserved Maria's copy of the *Remains*, he was not so particular with other reading material formerly owned by his wife. In a letter written to Hartley Coleridge, Charlotte described how, in her youth, she had "perused" the "antiquated print" of *The Lady's Magazine* – volumes she knew had belonged either to her aunt or mother – "as a treat on holiday afternoons or by stealth." This pleasure abruptly came to an end on *"one black day"* when her "father burnt them because they contained foolish love-stories."[28]

That act, if censorious, was in keeping with Patrick's steadfast religious principles. In his own evangelical tale, *The Cottage in the Wood*, Patrick had warned his readers against the "sensual novelist" and the "romantic author":

> *The sensual novelist and his admirer, are beings of depraved appetites and sickly imaginations, who having learnt the art of self-tormenting, are diligently and zealously employed in creating an imaginary world, which they can never inhabit, only to make the real world, with which they must necessarily be conversant, gloomy and insupportable ... The romantic author, overstepping the bounds of probability, will freely indulge in the miraculous.*[29]

Patrick's concern for his daughter's spiritual wellbeing must have outweighed any sentimental attachment he had to the magazines as former belongings of his departed wife.

---

27 Charles Bruce, ed. *The Book of Noble Englishwomen* (London and Edinburgh: William P. Nimmo, 1875), p. 386. N.B. The same account inaccurately records Patrick Brontë as having "picked up" the *Remains* from a wreck on the Yorkshire coast.

28 Charlotte Brontë, *The Letters of Charlotte Brontë*, ed. Margaret Smith, vol. 1: 1829-1847 (Oxford: Clarendon Press 1995): p. 240.

29 Brontë, Patrick. *The Cottage in the Wood; or the Art of Becoming Rich and Happy.* 2nd edition (Bradford: Printed for and sold by T. Inkersley, 1818), p. 3-4.

Patrick Brontë and Henry Kirke White both studied at St. John's College Cambridge.
Engraving by William Westall, 1815, reproduced by kind permission of the Master and Fellows of
St. John's College, Cambridge.

On the other hand, Patrick clearly approved of the contents of
the *Remains*. Patrick had enjoyed a personal connection with White
during their brief studies together at Cambridge. Like White, Patrick
had come from an impoverished family, and had attended St. John's
College as a sizar, arriving in 1802, just three years before White
began his studies there in 1805. Similar to White, Patrick had been
able to attend Cambridge thanks to the good offices of a Protestant
minister with strong Evangelical connections,[30] and both men were
ardent followers of Charles Simeon. The two young men had been
friendly acquaintances. Indeed, Patrick had shared information with
White about his own college expenses, so as to help White plan for
the ensuing financial pressures he would encounter at Cambridge.[31]

Although Patrick did not contribute a poem to the *Remains*,
he did note his association with the poet within his copy of the book.

30 Barker, *The Brontës*, p. 6.

31 Barker, *The Brontës*, 7-8. Southey includes a letter in the 1810 edition of the *Remains* that alludes to Patrick, but
does not mention him by name: "The Mr. * *, whose bills I have borrowed, has been at College three years. He
came over from * * with 10l. in his pocket, and has no friends or any income or emolument whatever, except
what he receives for his Sizarship" (vol. 1, p. 193).

On a front flyleaf of the *Remains* (trimmed during a later rebinding), Patrick had copied out in pencil the following praise about the *Remains* from a review initially published in *The Monthly Review* and later reprinted elsewhere:

> *[The][32] interesting subject of the volumes be[fore us] has bequeathed to us the most unques[tionable] proofs not only of some powers of mind [but] a disposition so gentle, amiable, benevo[lent and pious] that our regard for the loss of these [talents an]d qualities is enhanced by the per[suasion] that they would have been zealously [employed] in promoting the happiness, the vir[tue and] all the best interests of his fellow [crea]tures Monthly Review*

Patrick contributed his own testimony underneath in brown ink:

> *I had the honour of being acquainted at the University, with the subject of this memoir, and have every reason to think that the praise bestowed upon him, whether it respected him his genius or piety, — was well merited — P. Brontë*

In this way, Patrick added his own tribute to the *Remains*, in memory of his departed friend.

During its residence in the Brontë household, the *Remains* was probably stored with the bulk of Patrick's books in the Parsonage's study. Charlotte's close friend, Ellen Nussey, later recalled that there were "book-shelves in the Study but not many of them elsewhere."[33] The *Remains* would have resided there alongside copies of dictionaries and grammars, Bibles and concordances, religious tracts and moral tales (including Patrick's own published works), works of ancient literature in Latin and Greek,[34] works of science, history, arithmetic, geography, and philosophy, as well as works of English, French, and German literature. Perhaps the *Remains*

---

32 The text appearing in brackets was either sewn into the gutter of the book or trimmed from the fore-edge during the subsequent re-binding of the *Remains*.

33 Quoted in *The Brontës*, p. 100.

34 See Virgil. *The Works of Virgil Translated into English Verse*. London: Printed for C. and J. Rivington [&c.] by T. Davison, Whitefriars, 1824. bb64. The Brontë Parsonage Museum, Haworth, England.

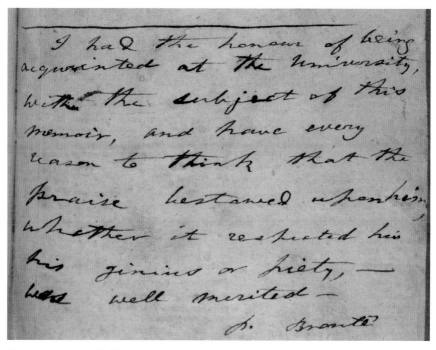

Patrick was proud of his own personal association with the deceased poet.

was shelved close to Patrick's prize books from Cambridge, among them editions of Horace and Homer. Or perhaps it was placed next to writings of the English Romantic poets, such as the family's set of Byron's complete works or the writings of Sir Walter Scott. Alternatively, the *Remains* may have been housed alongside books written by other evangelical poets, such as Hannah More, that were owned by the Brontës.

Regardless of where they were held within the library, both volumes of the *Remains* were heavily read and annotated by Patrick and his children with dozens of marks, including corrections, doodles, sums, marginal comments, and so on. Patrick was likely the reader who corrected *Giffard* to *Gifford* on page 24 of Southey's biography of White (Patrick would have studied William Gifford's translation of Juvenal at Cambridge, if not earlier). And Branwell is most likely to have drawn the large doodle of the head on page 314 of the second volume – an image that, incidentally, may have been a self-portrait, as it closely resembles his likeness. It was also probably Branwell who made the notes in cipher at the end of the second volume. Emily probably added the manicule (i.e., a pointing hand) in black ink in the margin of the poem *Solitude* adding the remark: "Kirk White's chef d'oeuvre."

Clearly, some of the Brontës were inspired by White's poems. In 1841, at the age of 24, Branwell wrote his poem *Lord Nelson* after "NELSONI. MORS. H. K. WHITE" as published in the *Remains*.[35] And at least one critic has suggested that Henry Kirke White's poem *Clifton Grove* may have informed the plot of *Wuthering Heights*.[36]

Charlotte seems to have been less influenced by White than her brother and sister. Although she admired Southey's poetry – heartily recommending it to her best friend, Ellen Nussey, along with the works of Milton, Shakespeare, Thompson, Goldsmith, Pope, Scott, Byron, Campbell, and Wordsworth[37] – Charlotte mentions neither White, nor his works, in her extant correspondence, nor does she allude to them in her novels. Rather, Charlotte was likely to have been more impressed by Southey's good offices in advancing the aims of White, a kindness that may well have prompted her to seek Southey's guidance in publishing her own poems. Having done so, she received a thoughtful reply from him, advising her:

> *Literature cannot be the business of a woman's life: & it ought not to be … But do not suppose that I disparage the gift wh you possess, nor that I wd. discourage you from exercising it, I only exhort you so to think of it & so to use it, as to render it conducive to your own permanent good. Write poetry for its own sake, not in a spirit of emulation, & not with a view to celebrity: the less you aim at that, the more likely you will be to deserve, & finally to obtain it.*[38]

35 Neufeldt, Victor A., ed. *The Works of Patrick Branwell Brontë: An Edition* vol. 3 of 3 volumes (New York and London: Garland Publishing, Inc., 1997), p. 354.

36 Richardson A. *The Lost Manuscripts* (The Brontë Society, 2018), pp. 132-174.

37 *Letters*, vol. 1, p. 130.

38 *Letters*, vol. 1, pp. 165-67.

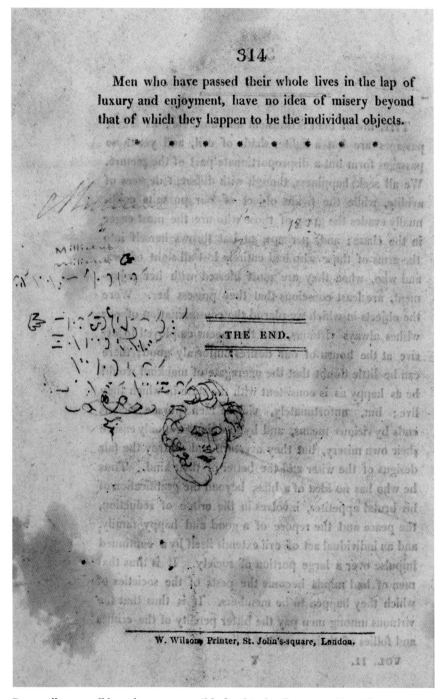

314

Men who have passed their whole lives in the lap of luxury and enjoyment, have no idea of misery beyond that of which they happen to be the individual objects.

THE END.

W. Wilson, Printer, St. John's-square, London.

Branwell may well have been responsible for this doodle, a possible self-portrait.

131

SOLITUDE.

IT is not that my lot is low,
That bids this silent tear to flow;
It is not grief that bids me moan,
It is that I am all alone.

In woods and glens I love to roam,
When the tir'd hedger hies him home;
Or by the woodland pool to rest,
When pale the star looks on its breast.

Yet when the silent evening sighs,
†With hallow'd airs and symphonies,
My spirit takes another tone,
And sighs that it is all alone.

The autumn leaf is sear and dead,
It floats upon the water's bed;
I would not be a leaf, to die
Without recording sorrow's sigh!

The woods and winds, with sudden wail,
Tell all the same unvaried tale;
I've none to smile when I am free,
And when I sigh, to sigh with me.

Yet in my dreams a form I view,
That thinks on me and loves me too;
I start, and when the vision's flown,
I weep that I am all alone.

K 2

Could this be Emily's marginal note?

Charlotte would follow Southey's advice, at least, in part. She wrote neither for celebrity, nor in a spirit of emulation. Nevertheless, ten years after she and Southey corresponded, 'Currer Bell' would become a household name. Indeed, Charlotte Brontë's reputation would increasingly grow, even as Henry Kirke White's reputation would diminish. By the end of the century, White was labeled as a "poetaster" in the *Dictionary of National Biography*.[39] By this time, *Jane Eyre* was available in countless editions, and had been widely adapted, translated, illustrated, and imitated by others, and "Charlotte Brontë" was a household name.

During Charlotte's lifetime, however, trauma followed fast on the heels of her swift success. Indeed, she would survive all of her siblings. Elizabeth and Maria had not lived past childhood. In 1848 – just a year after the publication of *Jane Eyre*, *Wuthering Heights*, and *Agnes Grey* – Branwell died at the age of 31, and then Emily at the age of 30. The following year, Anne died at the age of 29. Six years later, in 1855, Charlotte herself died at the age of 38.

It is tempting to entertain the idea that, before his own death in 1861, Patrick preserved Charlotte's juvenilia in the *Remains* to memorialise her work alongside that of his friend. After all, Charlotte, like Henry, had been a precocious writer as an adolescent. Charlotte had created dozens of small manuscript books whose seriffed letterforms imitated the contours of type. The fragments of Charlotte's juvenilia in the *Remains* – a leaf of poetry and a leaf of prose – attest to her early proclivity for writing. Patrick may have laid these fragments into the *Remains* to preserve them as evidence of his daughter's early genius. How fitting, too, for them to be preserved within a book once owned by his departed wife, and within a volume edited by Robert Southey, who had also corresponded with Charlotte in her youth.

As appealing to our own sensibilities as this scenario may be,

---

39 *Dictionary of National Biography*, ed. Sidney Lee, vol. 61 (New York: The Macmillan Company; London: Smith, Elder & Co., 1900), p. 48.

it is very unlikely. We are reminded of the following lines from Charlotte's second novel, *Shirley*:

> *Do you anticipate sentiment, and poetry, and reverie?*
> *Do you expect passion, and stimulus, and melodrama? Calm*
> *your expectations; reduce them to a lowly standard. Something*
> *real, cool, and solid, lies before you; something unromantic*
> *as Monday morning.*[40]

Indeed, the archaeology of this book – its physical construction, layers of content, and alteration over time – points to a very different narrative.

THE FIRST SALE AT AUCTION

The *Remains* was auctioned off quietly and without distinction on a Wednesday afternoon, October 2, 1861. The auction was occasioned by the impending departure of Arthur Bell Nicholls, Charlotte's widowed husband, from Haworth. Having served as Patrick's curate from 1845 to 1861, Nicholls had sought to succeed him as officiating minister of Haworth's church, St. Michael and All Angels. But the trustees of the church had voted against him in favour of John Wade, the vicar of Bradford's nominee.[41] As Nicholls prepared to leave Haworth, he hired the auctioneer, John Cragg, and his clerk (aptly named John Clark) to sell the remaining personal effects of Patrick Brontë at Haworth Parsonage.

The advertisement for the two-day auction featured Patrick's mahogany household furniture, including: "Eight Mahogany Chairs in Hair," "Two Mahogany Card Tables," a "Mahogany Dining Table," a "Mahogany Poll [sic] Screen" (i.e., a "pole" or fire screen), and a "Mahogany Rocking Chair," as well as "Kidderminster Carpets and Rugs," and so on.

---

40 Charlotte Bronte, *Shirley*, ed. Herbert Rosengarten and Margaret Smith (Oxford: Oxford University Press, 1979), p. 7.
41 Barker, *The Brontës*, pp. 822-825.

Patrick's framed engravings by John Martin – "The Deluge," "Belshazzar's Feast," and "Joshua commanding the Sun to stand" – were also highlighted for sale, along with other prints. The advertisement listed additional furniture, kitchenware, and glassware, as well as "about 200 vols. of BOOKS." All of the lots were available for viewing on Monday, September 30.[42] The surviving inventory of the sale, which includes a comprehensive list of the auction's lots and sale prices, makes no mention of the sale of any manuscripts.[43]

Toward the very end of the auction, the *Remains* was sold off with the other miscellaneous books constituting lot 51 to a "Mr Wood" for the price of 1s. 3d – something of a bargain. Although Charlotte was no longer living, she and her family members were celebrities, and a book annotated by Patrick and his children would have been of some interest. Elizabeth Gaskell's biography, published in 1857, had only amplified Charlotte's fame – and had also made public, for the first time, the fact that she and her siblings were the authors of a significant body of juvenilia – "wild weird writing," as Gaskell put it.

Nevertheless, had the *Remains* contained Charlotte's manuscript fragments at the time of the 1861 auction sale, both Nicholls and his auctioneers would surely have taken some notice. Indeed, it is extremely unlikely that Nicholls would have parted with them at all. Nicholls retained custody of the Brontë manuscripts for decades, writing in response to the historian Clement Shorter in 1895 that he still had them "in the bottom of a cupboard tied up in a newspaper, where they had lain for nearly 30 years."[44] It seems that, for his part, Nicholls had not made a regular habit of giving away manuscripts to autograph collectors. Nicholls did sell a number of manuscripts to Shorter for a small sum, believing that they would be placed in a London museum. Yet even then Nicholls retained a number of manuscripts that went to auction only after his death. Shorter,

42 "Notice of Sale of Household Furniture of Haworth Parsonage," P156, Brontë Parsonage Museum, Haworth, England.

43 "Sale by Auction at Howarth [sic] Parsonage," SB2008 and SB349, Brontë Parsonage Museum, Haworth, England.

44 Correspondence held as part of The Brotherton Collection, University of Leeds. Quoted in Clement Shorter's *Charlotte Brontë and Her Circle* (1896), p. 25.

meanwhile, brokered a deal, selling the manuscripts to the book collector – and forger – T. J. Wise, who dispersed them profitably, after having a number of them transcribed and printed as small press, limited editions.

With respect to the particular placement of Charlotte's manuscript fragments within the *Remains*, there is also the physical evidence supplied by the book itself. If the volumes were indeed "coverless" upon their sale at auction, as one source claims, then they would have made a flimsy enclosure for any letters or manuscript leaves. In addition, had Patrick added the manuscript leaves to the *Remains* himself, it would have been characteristic of him to document their significance, in the way that he had already assiduously recorded the book's provenance and his own past acquaintance with White. It was Patrick's custom to make such systematic notes. But none of the documentation about them is made in his hand.

Rather, in the Brontë's copy of the *Remains*, the majority of notes pertaining to the manuscripts are written in the hand of Reverend J. H. Wood, the same "Mr Wood" who had purchased the *Remains* at auction. Wood, a Baptist minister who resided in Haworth, had been acquainted with the Brontë family. It is his handwriting and initials that appear under the first specimen of Charlotte's early poetry:

> *Fragment of a poem by Charlotte Bronte and in her own hand writing JHW.*

Wood's note is written at the bottom of a crude paper frame into which the manuscript leaf had been inserted, so as to render both of its sides visible. The awkward mounting of the leaf within the flimsy frame seems like amateur work, perhaps by Wood himself. This presentation was clearly added to the book's printing matter as part of a new binding – for the frame, along with a series of additional leaves – appear following the volume's original endpapers

Left: Charlotte's poetry manuscript discovered within the leaves of the *Remains*.

and preliminary leaves (i.e., on one of which Patrick transcribed the aforementioned quotation from *The Monthly Review*, as well as documented his own account of White).

Wood took pains to interpret Charlotte's fragment of poetry. On a fresh leaf bound into the book and following the framed fragment, he attempted to transcribe Charlotte's miniscule writing, making the following note:

> *Transcript of the foregoing fragment as far as it can be made out.*

Arthur Bell Nicholls, Charlotte's husband, was custodian of the Brontës' effects following Patrick's death.

The tiny characters, written in pencil, were difficult for him to decipher, for his transcription is riddled with gaps.

Following this and bound into the book is yet another new leaf, its recto blank, and its verso inscribed as follows:

> *The writer of the following letter, Rev. Mr Nicholls, was the husband of Charlotte Bronte.*

Immediately following that insertion, and likewise bound into the book, is a letter that Nicholls had written to Wood in response to a condolence message that Wood had sent to Nicholls after

Charlotte's death. Nicholls' reply, written on black-bordered mourning stationery, reads as follows:

> *The Parsonage,*
> *Haworth.*
>
> *Rev. & Dear Sir,*
>
> On behalf of Mr Brontë &
> *myself I thank you sincerely for the sympathy expressed in your*
> *note for us under our recent bereavement—The affliction is indeed*
> *a heavy one, but we Endeavor to see in it the hand of our Heavenly*
> *Father, "who does not willingly afflict the children of men," & console*
> *ourselves by the reflection that our loss is her gain—*
> *Again thanking you for your kindness*
>
> *I am Rev. & Dr Sir*
> *Yrs faithfully,*
> *A. B. Nicholls*

Following this letter is yet another bound leaf, this time featuring a narrow manuscript fragment, tipped on to the recto of the leaf and written in cursive in brown ink. An annotation under this manuscript, written in pencil and in a new hand, attributes the specimen to Emily. It is a later hand than Wood's – one we will return to.

It still remains unclear as to how Wood acquired these remarkable leaves of Brontë juvenilia. The fragment of poetry is written in pencil, a circumstance that suggests it was a draft; the bulk of Charlotte's extant juvenilia consists of fair copy manuscripts written in dark brown ink (and often dated and signed). Was this leaf discarded by Charlotte and somehow salvaged by another person?

Alternatively, the two fragments of Charlotte's juvenilia may have been in Branwell's possession; he had often exchanged writing with Charlotte during their youth when the fragments were made. Careless in his final years, Branwell may have given them away, or possibly even exchanged them for a small sum. At the end of

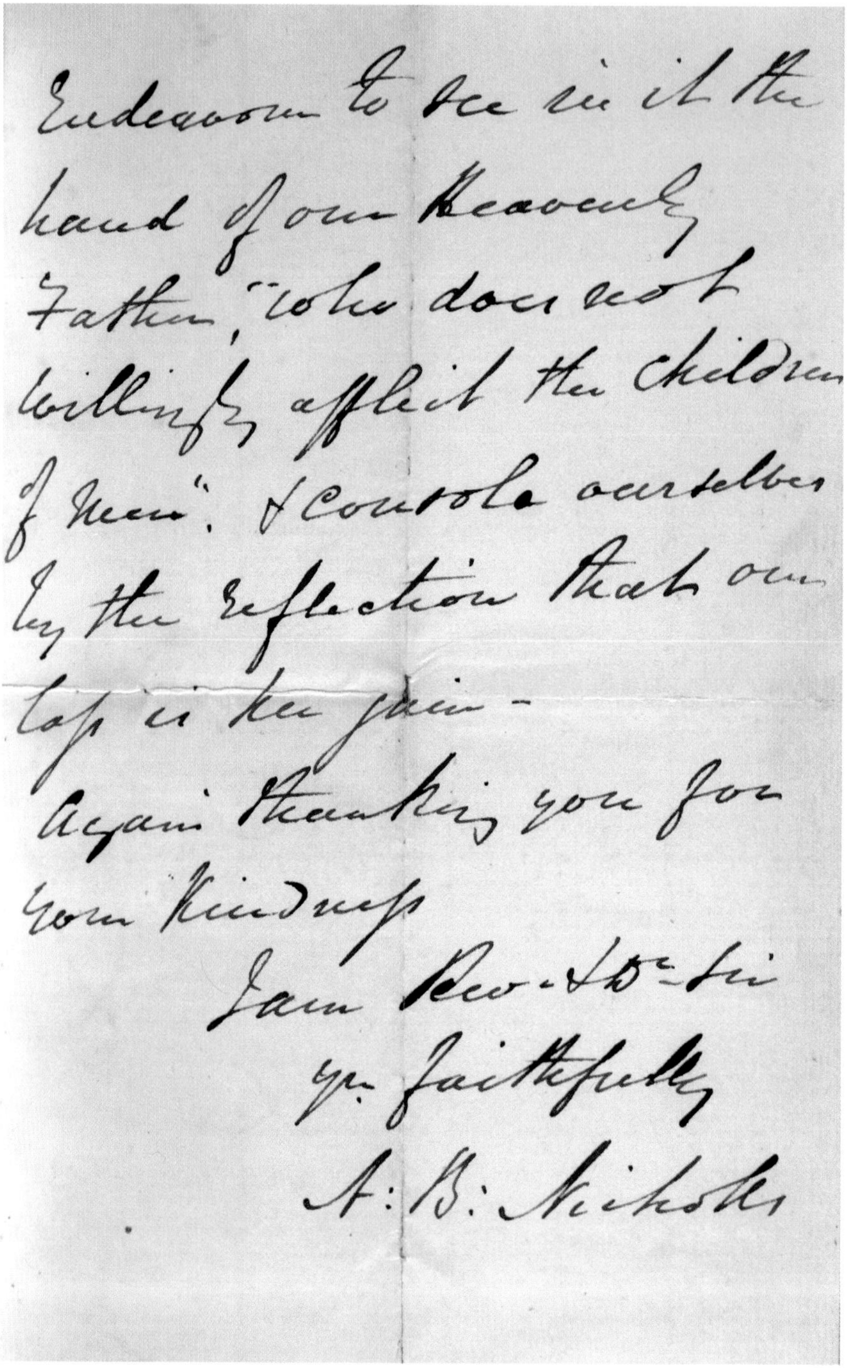

Endeavour to see in it the
hand of our Heavenly
Father, "who does not
willingly afflict the children
of Men". & console ourselves
by the reflection that our
loss is her gain —

Again thanking you for
your kindness

     I am Revᵈ & Dʳ Sir
     yrs faithfully
     A: B: Nicholls

Arthur Bell Nicholls' response to a letter of condolence following Charlotte's death.

his life, Branwell, an alcoholic, was deeply entrenched in debt and dependent on anyone who could supply him with money for liquor. Even in 1848, rumours were beginning to circulate in Yorkshire about the authorship of *Jane Eyre*.[45] In addition, there were the many letters and packages arriving at the Parsonage from London, as well as those being sent by Charlotte to her publishers, Smith, Elder. Although it is not clear that either Branwell or other residents of Haworth realised that Charlotte had published a novel (e.g., before his death in 1848[46]), Branwell's desperate need for cash and the concurrent rising interest in the identity of 'Currer Bell' together suggest the scenario as a possibility.

The content of Charlotte's prose fragment would have been of unusual interest to Wood, for it mentions Haworth by name,[47] as well as the Black Bull and also Keighley (the larger town adjacent to the village of Haworth). The fragment depicts Charlotte's fictionalised scribbling writer/anti-hero, Lord Charles Wellesley, "paying a visit" to Haworth in 1833 after being "driven from London by fear of his creditors." Accompanied by a Mr Thing, disguised as an itinerant Methodist minister, and operating under the alias "Charles Townshend," Wellesley "preached at the Wesleyan Chapel & contrived to embezzle the proceeds of the Quarterly Collection." Wellesley proceeds to attack Haworth's clergymen, including the Baptist minister, John Winterbottom (who, in life, frequently held liberal political views opposed by Patrick, a staunch Tory), before fleeing the town without paying his bill.

It is remarkable that Charlotte's early satirical treatment of Methodism – and of Patrick's Baptist opponent – was saved and later presented in the solemn context of the *Remains*. The fragment's

---

45 See Barker, pp. 562-564.

46 In a letter to W. S. Williams written in 1848, Charlotte claimed that Branwell "never knew what his sisters had done in literature—he was not aware that they had ever published a line." She writes, "we could not tell him of our efforts for fear of causing him too deep a pang of remorse for his own time misspent, and talents misapplied." *Letters*, vol. 2., pp. 122-23.

47 Christine Alexander, "Early Ambitions: Charlotte Brontë, Henry Kirke White and Robert Southey," *Brontë Studies*, 43:2, 14-31: 24.

irreverent, farcical treatment of dissenting religion offers a stark contrast to White's own earnest religious attitudes. The many layers of evidence in the *Remains*, including Wood's own transcription, clearly show that Wood studied the leaves closely and carefully. Taken as a whole, including these fragments and Patrick's inscriptions, the book's religious associations constitute their own compelling narrative.

THE JOURNEY FROM HAWORTH

At some point between 1861 and 1869, it seems that Wood had all of these materials bound together into one volume,[48] with the purpose of sending the collection to an acquaintance: the Reverend Edwin Paxton Hood. Before sending the book though, Wood added yet another layer of provenance to the increasingly complex *Remains* by inscribing the book to Hood as follows:

> *Purchased at the Sale of Mr. Brontë's effects and presented as a small token of gratitude esteem and affection to the Rev. E. P. Hood by his friend J. H. Wood.*

And so, after its residence there for more than forty years, the *Remains* finally left Haworth to reside with its new owner.

Largely forgotten now, Edwin Paxton Hood was a non-conformist minister well known in the nineteenth century as an editor, critic, and prolific writer of popular books. He served as the editor of *The Eclectic Review* and *The Argonaut*, and wrote a number of biographies ranging from the lives of famous English poets, such as Milton, Marvell, and Wordsworth, to those of other non-conformist ministers, including contemporaries and near-contemporaries Thomas Binney, Christmas Evans, and Robert Hall.[49]

Although Hood did not write a monograph on either the Brontës or Henry Kirke White, he certainly read – and very possibly reviewed

---

48 The wove papers on which the manuscript fragments were mounted and inscribed match one another; in addition, Rev. Hood's letter to Binney makes mention of the volumes of the book being bound together as a single volume.

49 *Dictionary of National Biography*, ed. Sidney Lee, vol. 27 (New York: The Macmillan Company; London: Smith, Elder & Co., 1900), p. 257.

– Gaskell's biography, *The Life of Charlotte Brontë* (London, 1857).[50] *The Eclectic Review*'s assessment of the *Life* includes a nuanced defence of the Reverend Carus Wilson's controversial management of Cowan Bridge School, where Charlotte and her older sisters, Maria and Elizabeth, had studied during a typhoid outbreak – the same institution that infamously served as the model for Lowood School in *Jane Eyre*. The unsigned review also emphasises Charlotte's own pious nature, and ends with a kind of homily, in keeping with Hood's own religious values:

> *God gave her great powers and many sorrows. But let not the sons and daughters of genius complain about their destiny, or wonder at it ... If they patiently endure their distresses, resolutely struggle against their difficulties, overcome troubles by holy strength and faith in God, instead of trying to forget them in wild self-indulgence, they will possess, when life comes to a close, a moral nature distinguished for power and beauty, as well as an intellect enriched with wealth and splendour.*[51]

If anything, the review sheds light on how Charlotte's works were received by contemporary evangelical readers – and why the Brontë copy of the *Remains*, with Charlotte's juvenilia, would have held a special interest for Hood and his clerical colleagues.

It may have been this review, or Hood's well-known interest in both religion and literary history, that motivated Wood to send him the *Remains*, containing Nicholls' letter and Charlotte's manuscripts, along with his own transcription and additional notes about the book. Hood, in turn, sent the volume on September 9, 1869 to his colleague (and the later subject of one of his biographies), Reverend Thomas Binney, the prominent Congregationalist minister of the King's Weigh House Chapel, London.

50 In Hood's correspondence to the Reverend Binney, he makes direct reference to Gaskell's biography: "in The front fly leaf old Mr. Brontes—(the father of Charlotte) Autograph we read much of Him in Mrs. Gaskells Life." Correspondence bound into the *Remains*.

51 *The Eclectic Review* (June 1857), 630-642: p. 642.

Born and raised in Newcastle upon Tyne, Binney's first job had been that of apprentice to a bookseller and printer by the name of George Angus. Angus's father, Thomas Angus, had specialised in printing chapbooks, and had employed the wood-engraver and illustrator, Thomas Bewick, at the outset of his illustrious career. This was, of course, the "Bewick" whose *History of British Birds* memorably appears in the opening pages of *Jane Eyre* – a connection that would have stood out to Binney.

Binney had the *Remains* for only a short time. For, sending the book to Binney, Hood writes:

> *Yours enclosing Dr Spragues letter came to hand on Saturday night too late for me to reply. The volume of Charlotte Brontes is so real a curiosity in the way of Autobiography. I should like you to see it before it goes to America I send it therefore at once to you.*

The *Remains* was destined for the collection of the Reverend William Buell Sprague (1795–1876), an American clergyman, evangelical writer, and voracious autograph collector – one of the leading collectors of the time. In this instance, Binney seems to have been acting as an agent for Sprague, introducing Hood to him in order to arrange for the book's international sale.[52] In his letter to Binney, Hood prominently mentions both fragments, but misattributes the prose fragment to Emily:

> *The other piece of writing is quite as curious or remarkable it is that of Emily Bronte. Even a still more extraordinary person than her sister she was the author of 'Wuthering Heights'.*

If all four evangelical clergyman – Wood, Hood, Binney, and Sprague – were fascinated by the *Remains*, Sprague had both the greater resources and the larger appetite for antiquarian books and manuscripts. A contemporary account reputedly wrote that Sprague had:

---

52 In Hood's correspondence to Binney, he indicates that Binney had sent him a letter enclosing a letter from Sprague.

so much fury about him in collecting autographs that he would
carry off everything that had a name attached to it.[53]

It is also quite possible that Hood may have routinely procured rare
books with famous religious and literary associations in England for
Sprague. In his letter to Binney, Hood mentions not one, but three
rare, antiquarian books: the second book being a Bible that Charlotte
used at St. Michael's Church at Haworth, and the third being another
book with an illustrious (and also clerical) connection. Hood writes:

> *my wife was visiting there—& on the Sabbath afternoon sat in*
> *the Bronte pew & used Charlotte's book, & footstool. Mr Nicholls*
> *preached—then I think she rec'd this book—I enclose these* [i.e., the
> *Remains* and the Bible] *& also if Dr Sprague will accept thru you*
> *a volume every whit whit as curious formerly the Property of Dean*
> *Swift—containing his Autograph in the front fly page—& his notes*
> *throughout the volume.*

The book was a copy of *Medulla Historiae Anglicanae: The Ancient
and Present State of England* (9th edition, London 1734).[54] It had
been given by Swift to his second cousin, Mary Harrison, in 1736,
with the following inscription: "to encourage her to read usefull and
improving Books."[55]

The *Remains*, Charlotte's Bible, and the *Medulla* were shipped
(this time, safely) to Sprague's residence in Albany, New York.
Sprague, who was the author of more than 100 publications,
including sermons, essays, and addresses, apparently did nothing
by halves. The *Remains* joined a vast collection that is said to have
contained 100,000 autographs.[56] But Sprague, who was already

53 Quoted in Francis Manley's article, "Swift Marginalia in Howell's *Medulla Historiae Anglicanae*," *PMLA* (73),
   no. 4, part 1 (September 1958): pp. 335-338.

54 The book now resides at the Milton S. Eisenhower Library of The Johns Hopkins University in Baltimore,
   Maryland. Its call number is DA32 .H85 1734R c. 1.

55 Manley, "Swift Marginalia in Howell's *Medulla Historiae Anglicanae*", p. 335.

56 Entry for "William Buell Sprague." *Appletons' Cyclopedia of American Biography*, eds. John Grant Wilson and
   John Fiske, vol. 5 (New York: D. Appleton and Company, 188), p. 168.

advanced in years, would not build his library for much longer. He died in 1876 at the age of 80.

The *Remains* was auctioned off in May of 1878 in New York City by Bangs & Company as part of the "concluding portion" of the sale of Sprague's vast collection. The catalogue was advertised as featuring "books with rare autographs," as well as "many rare and interesting books in various departments of literature, American history, and biography." (It also contains a description of the Swift copy of the *Medulla*, featured as lot 318.) The *Remains* was lot 678, described as "2 vols. in 1," bound in a single half-calf binding. The brief description of the lot mentions Charlotte's fragment, as well as Nicholls' letter, Patrick's inscriptions, and Hood's correspondence.

From this point on, the book moved from the hands of book-collecting clergymen into those of collectors specialising in nineteenth-century British literature, annotated books, and so-called 'Grangerized books,' or books extra-illustrated with prints, correspondence, and related ephemera. It is almost certain that the man who purchased the *Remains* at the Sprague sale was the Chicago businessman John A. Spoor (1851–1926). At that time, Spoor would have been 26, and already an avid collector of nineteenth-century English poets and essayists.

By the time of his death, Spoor's collection featured breath-taking rarities, including a copybook containing manuscript notes by Percy Bysshe Shelley and Mary Shelley, and also an autograph album inscribed by Keats, Southey, Tennyson, and Wordsworth.[57] Spoor also collected Brontëana. His copy of the "Bell's" *Poems* was one of the scarce first issues of the book, bound in the publishers' original light green cloth binding, with a letter laid in from Charlotte to her publishers, Aylott and Jones, acknowledging the receipt of two copies of *Poems*, and complimenting them on the books' *"very neat"* bindings.[58] The copy, recently sold at auction to an American

57 Donald C. Dickinson, *Dictionary of American Book Collectors* (New York; Westport, Connecticut; London: Greenwood Press, 1986), pp. 293-94.

58 Smith, *Letters*, vol. 1., pp. 499-500.

collector, contains Spoor's bookplate.[59]

It is certainly Spoor's initials – *"JAS"* – that sign a note laid into the book recounting its provenance through his own acquisition (*"Bought by me at the sale of Mr. Sprague's library"*). It also appears to be Spoor who annotated Charlotte's prose fragment as follows:

> *This is in Emily Bronte's handwriting. See Letter of Rev. E. P. Hood bound in back of the volume.*

Most probably, Spoor would have also pasted into the book the 1886 newspaper clipping from *The New York Times* announcing *BRONTE RELICS SOLD*.

It was either Spoor, or the book's subsequent owner, Judge Joseph F. Daly, who had the book rebound in its current deluxe binding by Haddon & Company, a bookbinder active in New York City during the last quarter of the nineteenth century. The binders' names are stamped on an outer edge of the back pastedown. A major collector, Spoor could easily have commissioned it, given his great wealth and the grandeur of his collection. But Daly, who acquired the book either directly from Spoor or through an agent of Spoor's at an unknown point in time before Daly's death in 1916, was also known to commission custom bindings for his books. As Anderson Galleries' auction catalogue notes:

> *Judge Daly was not a book collector as the term is frequently used; he bought in order to read, and if reading created a permanent interest the volumes were properly bound, and were frequently extra-illustrated with rare engravings, mainly portraits.*

A highlight of the Daly sale, the Brontë copy of the *Remains* was noted as holding "first place" among the many association copies in Daly's collection "for the personal note in Charlotte Brontë's copy."[60]

---

59 See lot 330 as part of the auction, "Fine Books, Manuscripts and Works on Paper," Forum Auctions, 10 July 2017: https://www.forumauctions.co.uk/32406/Brone-sisters-Poems-1st-ed.-1st-issue-1846-with-ALs-from-Charlotte-Bronte-tipped-in?auction_no=1013&view=lot_detail

60 Anderson Galleries, "BRONTE SOUVENIR," on Tuesday afternoon 5 and 6 December 1916 as part of sale 1255, "Catalogue of the Fine Library of the Late Judge Joseph F. Daly of New York: Rarities in Many Departments of Literature, Extra-illustrated Books, including Ireland's New York Stage, and Hundreds of Rare Engravings."

The book, with its "collateral proof" and "pedigree," was billed as BRONTE SOUVENIR, and was sold in December of 1916 as lot 84 for a hammer price of $245,[61] a real value equivalent of approximately $11,300 in 2018 currency.[62] The purchaser was Mary McMillin Norton – another collector of extra-illustrated books and association copies.

Norton's collection included a wide range of manuscripts, from a fifteenth century French *Book of Hours*, to two Twain manuscripts, with a cache of Byron manuscripts in between. Like the collectors of the *Remains* preceding her, she was keenly interested in autographs. For instance, she owned a collection of autographs made by past Presidents of the United States (from Washington to Wilson), as well as a copy of Tennyson's *Demeter and Other Poems* (London, 1889) containing a pasted-in autograph note by Tennyson to his publisher. Notably, she did not own any other Brontë material.

Norton did not hold on to the *Remains* for long. She sold her collection in 1918 through Anderson Galleries, where she had acquired the book just two years before. The *Remains* was sold alongside Norton's set of four Shakespeare folios, as well as other notable books, including John Ruskin's copy of the *Nuremberg Chronicle*, containing fifteenth- and sixteenth-century marginalia and annotations. The *Remains* sold for $200 – $45 less than it had in 1916 – to an anonymous family who held it for nearly one hundred years, before offering it for sale through Randall House Rare Books.

RETURNING HOME

In 2016, the Brontë Parsonage Museum purchased the book for a six figure sum – exactly a thousand times the cost of its 1918 auction price. Thus, the *Remains* finally returned to Haworth after its long residence abroad.

When a book such as the *Remains*, finally makes its way into a museum or library, there is a sense of closure. The book leaves

---

61   See *American Book Prices Current*.

62   Lawrence H. Officer and Samuel H. Williamson, "Five Ways to Compute the Relative Value of a UK Pound Amount, 1270 to Present," MeasuringWorth, 2018.

a private home, and enters a public institution. The book's location is known and established. It can be consulted by scholars, displayed by curators, and interpreted alongside other like objects within the collection – in this case, the remarkable contents of the Brontë Parsonage Museum.

What we so often lose when an artefact settles into a museum, however, are the stories of its prior owners. So many books have witnessed and endured extraordinary events as part of their lives in private collections but usually, over time, those histories are eventually lost, effaced, overlooked, or forgotten, along with the rich details of the other objects and private lives that were touched, and perhaps even shaped, by one that no longer resides among them. Such associations inform the life of any book. In this case, Howell's *Medulla Historiae Anglicanae*, which had been annotated by Jonathan Swift and which once travelled together with the *Remains*, revealed certain intellectual resonances valued by nineteenth century evangelical scholar-collectors. When Sprague's collection was auctioned off, that important historical link was severed, but for Hood's letter to Binney, bound within the book.

The *Remains* is a remarkable object, finally, because its former owners embedded so much of themselves within its pages: their histories, their scholarship, their values, and, ultimately, their desire for an enduring bond to the book itself as a physical object. Few artefacts can supply so much evidence either of their provenance or their travels. Every inscription in the *Remains* – every layer bound within its covers – points to a constellation of related collections, individuals, and ideas. Neither bones in a grave nor ashes in an urn, these histories persist in the *Remains*.

A VISIT TO HAWORTH

Emma Butcher

Merging fantasy with reality

In June 1833, Charlotte Brontë invited her fictionalised Glass Town character, Charles Townshend, for a jaunt in Haworth. Throughout their childhood years the Brontë siblings created magical worlds, building detailed metropolises inhabited with a variety of characters ranging from the rich aristocracy to 'rarelads', the thieves, drunkards and underbelly of society.

Until now, their two worlds of reality and fantasy have remained entirely separate. Yet, for the first time, this manuscript shows that Charlotte introduced her imaginary realm to her local village.

This essay explores this interesting encounter and draws on some of the key themes that make the Brontë's juvenilia a truly exceptional body of writing.

Dr Emma Butcher is a Leverhulme Early Career Researcher at the University of Leicester. In 2017 she was named as a BBC New Generation Thinker, and has written and spoken on the Brontës for BBC2, BBC Radio 3, and *The Guardian*. In 2015, she co-curated the Brontë Parsonage Museum's exhibition, *The Brontës, War and Waterloo*. Her monograph, *The Brontës and War*, will be published by Palgrave Macmillan in 2019.

The discovery of a new juvenilia manuscript written by Charlotte Brontë in Mrs Brontë's copy of *The Remains of Henry Kirke White* is very special. Although short, it is filled with fun, bawdiness, and violence, all taking place in the Brontës' hometown of Haworth. Written in 1833, it is positioned at the beginning of a burgeoning creative period in Charlotte's young writing life. Here it is, presented in full:

[Untitled] A VISIT TO HAWORTH

June 1833, Lord C Wellesley paid a visit to Haworth, being driven from London by fear of his creditors, He took up his quarters at the Black Bull where he excited much attention by his manners and appearance which were not such as are often seen in a country village, by his regular absence during the day & his equally regular return as night fell generally accompanied by a company of the very riff raff of the place whom it was his delight to fill with as much drink as they could hold and then witness and sometimes participate in the quarrels which arose out of their inebriety. He went by the name of Charles Townshend Esqr. And was usually to be seen in the society of a little old man of most suspicious aspect whom he called Mr Robert Thing These brothers passed themselves off for two ...

Right: The first page of Charlotte's prose manuscript found within the pages of Mrs Brontë's book.

In June 1833, Lord C____
off Me by Desire on
visit to Howarth
being driven from home
sometime by fear of his
creditors, He took up
his quarters at the
Black Bull Inn here
he excited much at-
tention by his manner
and appearance which
were not such as are
often seen in a
Yorkshire village, by
his regular absence during
the day & his equally
regular return at Night
fall, generally accom-
panied by the very rift
raff of the place, whom
it was his delight to
fill with as much
drink as they could
hold and then witness
& sometimes participate
in the quarrels which
were out of their
inebriety. He was at-
tended by a man
the Name of Charles Town—
land Esq. & was usually
to be seen in the
society of a little, ill
Name of Dr____ surgeon
called Dr Robert King
These worthies passed
themselves off for two

Primitives in the Methodist
Connection &c. one time
Mr Townshend preached
at the Wesleyan Chapel
& contrived to embezzle
the proceeds of the
Quarterly Collection. He
likewise in company
with Mr Phing broke
into the house of the
Rev John Winterbottom
in the middle of the
night, dragged him
from his bed, & had
him drawn by the heels
from one end of the
village to the other.
Subsequently he stucked
John Foster the Minister
of &c. in a horse pond
half sunk. Mr Robson
the Methodist Preacher
he publicly flogged
Mr John Hartley being
fixed up the put it
James Greenwood Esqr
in the open street &
frightened Mr Sunderland
Organist of Keighley
into temporary insanity
& after the commission of
all these enormities made
a moonlight flitting from
the Black Bull without
paying a stiver of his
reckoning.

... ministers in the Methodist connection at one time Mr Townshend
preached at the Wesleyan Chapel & contrived to embezzle the proceeds
of the Quarterley Collection. He likewise in company with Mr Thing
broke into the house of the Revd John Winterbottom in the middle of the
night, dragged him from his bed, & had him drawn by the heels from
one end of the village to the other. Subsequently he ducked John Foster
[?] the [?] of [?] in a horse pond half hung Mr Robson the Methodist
Preacher Then publicly flogged Mr John Hartley, tripped up the feet of
James Greenwood Esqr. in the open streets, frightened Mr Sunderland
Organist of Keighley into temporary insanity & after the commission
of all these enormities made a moonlight flitting from the Black Bull
without paying a sliver of his reckoning.

THE JUVENILIA

Before we move into the specifics of the manuscript, we must
consider the context of the juvenilia, and its importance as a whole
to Brontë studies.

What most of us have read of the Brontës is only the tip of the
iceberg. Before the three sisters penned their successful literary
debuts, the four siblings – Charlotte, Emily, Anne, and Branwell
– were already a writing powerhouse. From 1826, when their father
brought home a box of toy soldiers, they collaborated on fantasy
worlds that brought their toys to life. Together, they created
fantastical kingdoms and populated them with a series of characters
and events. Combined, the details and complexities of their worlds
rival the most famous literary kingdoms in English literature.

The Brontës' youthful literature is notoriously difficult to navigate.
Initially, between the years of 1826 and 1832, all four siblings
contributed to the same collective dramas, culminating with the Glass
Town saga, set in the exotic West Coast of Africa. Then, in 1832, Emily
and Anne broke away from Charlotte and Branwell to form their
own kingdom, which they named Gondal. Although we are uncertain

Left: The story continues on a second page, pasted inside the *Remains*.

as to why this happened, it is clear that the two younger sisters were not given much input into the foursome's adventures. None of the manuscripts demonstrate their hand. After Emily and Anne's departure, Charlotte and Branwell continued to collaborate, expanding their Glass Town Empire into a new kingdom, which they called Angria. They wrote dual narratives until 1839, both siblings often reacting to stories the other produced. In 1839, Charlotte wrote her final Angrian manuscript, *Farewell to Angria*, bidding goodbye to her fantasy world and committing to different literary ventures. Branwell continued to write Angrian stories and verse until his death in 1848.

As can be deduced from this potted timeline, the juvenilia are almost a parallel universe to the siblings' lives. The plots, characters, and settings are recognisable to us as mutations of the past. For example, the Duke of Wellington and Napoleon exist within the saga, gradually morphing into the Byronic Duke of Zamorna, King of Angria, and demonic Alexander Percy, Prime Minister of Angria. The siblings were historically aware within their work, using popular books and periodicals of the day to inform their stories. Despite their scholarly foundations, however, the saga's purpose was not to reflect the world around them. It was an exercise in escapism, where the limits of the universe could be tested and spiritual forces and extremities of human emotion could be explored to their full extent.

Charlotte and Branwell wrote the majority of their manuscripts in miniature hand, almost illegible to the naked eye. Some of their early writings mimicked the magazine culture of their day, constructing miniature periodicals – including features, poetry, and conversations – from potato sacks. Other fully formed stories would be written out normally but still in minute hand. But why the secrecy?

In order to consider this question we must think of the siblings' positions. Their father was a respected curate, who, conveniently for them, had very poor eyesight. Their stories, which included adult themes and explicit content – sex, war, violence – were never intended to be read by a public audience, but kept contained within their writing workshop. Although their father may have been a little naïve as to the content of these stories, he was supportive, opening his entire library to his children and encouraging them to read.

Charlotte in particular mastered the skill of characterisation in her early years. Whereas her brother, Branwell, invested his time writing war epics and parliamentary speeches, Charlotte was interested in exploring the psychology and relationships of her Glass Town and Angrian characters. Her stories are character driven and it is clear that by the 1830s she had become emotionally invested in her fantasy world and that it was becoming inextricably bound with her own selfhood. In her *Roe Head Journal*, written during her time as an assistant teacher at Miss Wooler's school for young ladies, she made a confession: she much preferred the company of her imaginary friends than engaging in the real world around her:

It is that which wakes my spirit & engrosses all my living feelings, all my energies which are not merely mechanical & like Haworth & home wakes sensations which lie dormant elsewhere. Last night I did indeed lean upon the thunder-wakening wings of such a stormy blast as I have seldom heard blow & it whirled me away like heath in the wilderness for five seconds of ectasy – and as I sat by myself in the dining-room while all the rest were at tea the trance seemed to descend on a sudden & verily this foot trod the war-shaken shores of the Calabar [. . .] I went to the wall of the palace to the line of latticed arches which shimmered in light, passing along quick as thought I glanced at what the internal glare revealed through the crystal, there was a room lined with mirrors & with lamps on tripods & very decorated [?] & splendid couches & carpets & large half lucid vases white as snow, thickly embossed with whiter mouldings & one large picture in a frame of massive beauty representing a young man [Zamorna] whose gorgeous & shining locks seemed as if they would wave on the breath.

Charlotte's passion is clear, and we cannot help but be transported with her. She could so easily blend fantasy and reality; tumbling effortlessly into daydream. This is, perhaps, why she ended her relationship with her fantasy world. By the late 1830s, while Branwell was beginning his descent into drunken oblivion, Charlotte chose to rise from fantasy and begin work on writings that could be published. In short, she feared she would go mad, so she said goodbye to her characters, scenes and subjects. Charlotte imagined her beautiful kingdom, in "every variety of shade and light which morning, noon and evening – the rising, the meridian & the setting sun – can bestow upon them",[1] and she wrote of the pain she felt at wrenching herself from her "friends" and venturing into lands unknown – "I feel almost as if I stood on the threshold of a home and were bidding farewell to its inmates."[2]

It is at this point that we believe Charlotte returned to Haworth, trading her exotic African landscape for literary inspiration closer to home. Think, for instance, of *Jane Eyre*'s Thornfield and *Shirley*'s Spen Valley. What we thought we knew up until now has, however, been incorrect. This new juvenilia manuscript shows for the first time that Charlotte invited her imaginary realm to her local village, hosting her metropolitan, bawdy characters within her local, very much loved stomping ground.

JUNE 1833: A TIME OF CHANGE AND EXPERIMENTATION

Far from being secluded from the outside world, the small town of Haworth was becoming the setting for social and religious change, with an influx of new ideas, both cultural and political. Branwell became a pupil of the portrait painter, William Robinson, and the Reverend Patrick Brontë joined Keighley Mechanics Institute, gaining access to its lectures, library and reading room. The social fabric of the local area was undergoing major upheavals as new

---

1 'Farewell to Angria'. See Christine Alexander's *Tales of Glass Town, Angria and Gondal*, p. 314.

2 Ibid.

factory acts restricted children's working hours in the local mills. The religious fabric of the country was also shifting. The Oxford Movement saw the beginnings of a Catholic revival in the Anglican Church, and its associated Tractarian philosophy was being published. At the same time, the Revd. Brontë was struggling to negotiate relations between the Established Church and the Dissenters, and funds for the Auxiliary of the Bible Society suffered.

In the Brontë siblings' fantasy worlds, 1833 was a significant year. Whilst Emily and Anne were busy building Gondal, Branwell and Charlotte were expanding their Glass Town saga. Branwell spent the majority of the year developing his character, Alexander Percy, in tales such as *The Pirate* and *Real Life in Verdopolis*, and exploring the saga's political and social allegiances in tales such as *The Politics of Verdopolis*. Charlotte responded to Branwell's writings, using the changes he initiated as a platform for her own events, and for her characters' relationships. They were working in unison: their shared motivation and creative consciousness almost anticipates the climactic evolution of their kingdom into Angria the following year.

Although 1831 and 1832 saw a relatively dry spell for Charlotte whilst she was an assistant teacher at Roe Head School, 1833 saw her writing talents flourish once more. In February she wrote *The African Queen's Lament*, a poem about the tragic fate of Quashia Quamina's mother, the native Ashantee Queen. In May, she wrote *Something About Arthur*, a tale of horse betting, mill attacks, and the budding relationship between the 15-year-old Marquis of Douro (later Zamorna) and his later mistress, Mina Laury. Throughout June, Charlotte wrote her most complex story to date, *The Foundling*. This tale interweaves Glass Town's history alongside the siblings' developing saga. The protagonist of the tale, Edward Sydney, learns of his true identity as Prince Edward of York, son of the Duke of York who, along with eleven other men, sailed from England to colonise Glass Town. After this tale, Charlotte's writing pace increased, producing some of her great juvenilia tales: *The Green*

Dwarf, the *Arthuriana* collection, *The Secret*, and *Lily Hart*. One tale, *The Vision*, produced in October of 1833 has never been found, yet promises to hold the same attention to detail as her other stories.

It is no surprise then, that a new juvenilia story is discovered within this productive period of Charlotte's writing life. The story is exciting, bawdy, and daring, following a trope in popular literature that Charlotte and Branwell both read and adapted: the silver fork novel. The genre saw great popularity between the 1820s and the 1840s and principally concerned the habits and scandals of the elite, which would have been titillating and shocking to the rising respectable middle classes. The Brontë juvenilia's relationship with the silver fork novel has been explored by numerous academics such as Glen, Nyborg, Wager.[3] They may have read popular volumes of the present day, such as Edward Bulwer Lytton's *Pelham: Or the Adventures of a Gentleman* (1828), which contained violent scenes of fisticuffs and duels. This influence is especially felt in Charlotte's stories of 1833: her tales *Something About Arthur* and *The Post Office*, for example, see fisticuffs and drunken, debauched scenes. The latter describes a great party at Mr Bellingham's, a rich banker, where "rare lads", the lower class underbelly of Glass Town, gate-crash the indulgent event leaving alcohol-infused chaos in their wake – "Shattered glass and porcelain, spilt wine, crushed and trampled sweetmeats, broken furniture and torn tapestry".[4]

Branwell also drew influence from the genre in his 1833 stories. For example, in his tale, *Brushwood Hall* – a short piece within his larger work *The Monthly Intelligencer* – Alexander Percy, currently known as 'Rogue', and his wife Zenobia host a party that concludes with a fight where a "whole array of combatants with. Blackened faces bloody noses blind [eyes and]. Torn coats marched behind their silken sovereigns into the supper [room]".[5]

3   See Heather Glen's 'Introduction' in *Tales from Angria* (2006), and Erin Nyborg's and Tamama Silvia Wagner's essays in *Charlotte Brontë: From the Beginnings* (2016).

4   EEW II 1991, p. 215.

5   WPBB I 1997, p. 253.

Zenobia, wife of Branwell's fictitious character, Alexander Percy.

It is clear that both siblings took great delight in tarnishing the reputations of their aristocratic characters within the safety of their stately homes.

In a similar vein, the newly discovered manuscript is concerned with upper class vices. Charlotte's chosen character, Lord Charles Wellesley, is the aristocratic younger brother of the Duke of Zamorna, the king and hero of the saga. Although this character may seem like the perfect muse for a silver fork tale, Charlotte's representation of Charles as a bawdy drunkard is, in fact, highly unusual. Generally, she presents him as a spectator, spying on his brother's scandalous antics and reporting on them. How interesting, then, that Charlotte chose his solo adventure to Haworth as a time for him to revel in the very antics he usually criticises. Still more interesting is Charlotte's

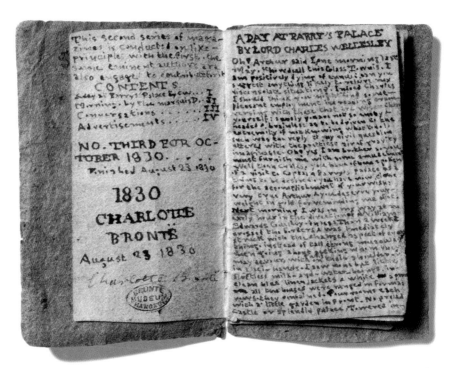

Title page from *The Young Men's Magazine*, written by Charlotte in August 1830 and featuring her hero, Lord Charles Wellesley.

choice of name for him. Although he is initially introduced as Lord C. Wellesley, he later goes by the name of Charles Townshend. This trend of renaming and rewriting characters is not unknown in the Brontë juvenilia, yet the timing here is significant.

In Charlotte's writings between 1829 and 1837, Charles is painted as a young, annoying, yet observant little brother, trying to target his older brother in a cat and mouse game of sibling politics. Brontë scholar, Christine Alexander, has noted that Charlotte often struggled to negotiate Charles' young age with his satirical, urbane attitude.[6] Yet, in her tale *Passing Events*, written in 1837, Charlotte renames Charles Wellesley as Charles Townshend, now a 20-year-old dandy, whose criticisms are directed at his brother's social circle rather than focusing on his brother himself. How strange that this new, reinvented character appears in the new manuscript some four years before his supposed first appearance.

6   See Christine Alexander and Margaret Smith, *Oxford Companion to the Brontës*, p. 533.

At this very early period in her writing career, it is clear that seventeen-year-old Charlotte is already exhibiting signs of the writing maturity that is demonstrated in her later juvenilia manuscripts and her adult works. She is thinking carefully about her character's personality within the saga, using the freedom of her world to release him from the shackles of his former identity, and exploring how his role develops. The new manuscript can be seen as an experiment in reinvention.

HAWORTH AND ITS PEOPLE

It was typical for the siblings to draw from real life events, people, and literature in their juvenilia, but this is the first manuscript where both Glass Town and Haworth merge. Let's start with setting. The story begins with Charles arriving in Haworth from London. London was, for the young Brontës, a dazzling metropolis that was populated with aristocratic, eminent men, such as the Duke of Wellington. Their Glass Town world, specifically cities such as Verdopolis, was partially modelled on its architecture, including its vast open parks, and buzzing population. It is therefore not so much of a jump for Charlotte's Lord to arrive from a recognisable, realistic, location. To the Brontës, London was as much a dreamscape as their own imaginative realm.

London is not, however, the main setting of this story. Very quickly we are transported to a familiar location: Haworth, specifically the Black Bull. The 'Bull' was one of the central inns and drinking houses in Haworth. It was Branwell's alehouse of choice in the village and he was popular with both the staff and his fellow patrons. This safe refuge, which would ultimately contribute to his alcohol-infused downfall, has become a part of the Brontë story.

Tales about goings-on in the Black Bull have gone down in history, including the time when Branwell and other villagers temporarily imprisoned Luddite rioters within its walls after they had sabotaged nearby work machinery. It was also reported that in the eighteenth century, the Reverend William Grimshaw would run into the pub and whip regular boozers into church. Until 1833, the year of this manuscript, meetings of the Three Graces Masonic Lodge were held within this gritstone building. Branwell would later become a member in 1836; his Masonic apron, which is covered in emblematic Freemason imagery, forms part of a private collection recently on loan to the Brontë Parsonage Museum. From these select stories, it is clear that the Black Bull became an iconic symbol of decadence, bawdiness, and frivolity. No doubt, countless tales and sightings of its drunken inhabitants would have filled Charlotte's mind when she talks of "the place whom it was a delight to fill with as much drink

The Black Bull in Haworth, the drinking house frequented by Branwell, pictured in 1856.

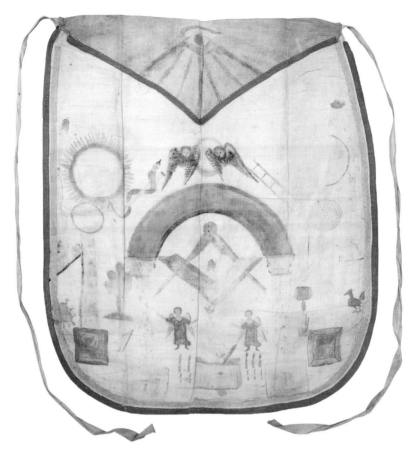

The Masonic apron, painted by Branwell when he was a member of the Haworth Lodge.
On loan from Nigel Thomas Carlton of the Thomas family

as they could hold and then witness and sometimes participate in the quarrels which arose out of their inebriety". It was the perfect setting for the mingling and raucous behaviour of "riff raff", or "rare lads", and naughty aristocrats.

The main body of the story is concerned with Charles and Mr Robert Thing, an unknown character, terrorising the residents of Haworth by posing as Methodists, or Dissenters. As we know, the Brontës' father had a problematic relationship with this divisive strand of Christianity, especially in 1833 when rebellions were rife in the local area. Charlotte, like Branwell in his Glass Town writings,[7]

7   See, for example, Branwell's final extended writing venture before his death: *And the Weary are at Rest* (1845).

treated Methodism with a hint of satire, though for her it also generated an anxiety, on a par with her father. The very name, Charles Wellesley, is similar to the founding name of Methodism, Wesley. Charles Wesley, brother of the founder, John Wesley, was one of the first members of the strand, contributing to his brother's cause by preaching and writing hymns. The hymns are mocked in Charlotte's novel, *Shirley* (1849), her narrator noting surprise that the Methodist church roof did not fly off with the frantic cries of its worshippers.

In this newly discovered manuscript, Charles is presented as a crooked fraud, alongside Thing, who is described as his brother, perhaps referring to and imitating the founder, John. Together, they preach and embezzle money, reflecting Charlotte's distrust and unease of Methodism. Although differing in a number of ways, the tone and themes of the manuscript bring to mind an earlier tale of Charlotte's, *An Interesting Passage in the Lives of Some Eminent Men of the Present Time* (1830). This sensational tale sees a scandalous robbery of library books by Glass Town's literary society, which are being stored in coffins in a large vault within the cemetery. In this manuscript, however, books are money, and literature is religion.

The final section of the manuscript introduces an array of new characters: but, for the first time, these are not Charlotte's imaginary friends, but the real-life residents of Haworth, transmogrified into the young sibling's saga. Winterbottom – or, Winterbot[h]am – was the Baptist minister of the West Lane Baptist Chapel. Although he co-operated with the Reverend Patrick Brontë on many village projects, he was a fierce opponent on topics such as church rates. In 1834, Patrick would write of his displeasure at his opposition in the local *Leeds Intelligencer*.

The names [W] Foster, [William] Hartley and [John, W. C.] Greenwood were also familiar names in Haworth and all members of the Three Graces Lodge Freemasons society. Hartley was the name of several families in the village: James Hartley was the first minister of the West Lane Baptist Church in 1752, Joseph Hartley

The Methodist Chapel in Haworth: the Reverend William Grimshaw's original Wesleyan Methodist Chapel was replaced by this building in 1846. It seated 650, and was later extended in 1853.

West Lane Baptist Chapel, Haworth: this building dates from 1845 – the first Baptist Chapel in Haworth was founded in 1752.

Bridgehouse Mill, one of the ten spinning mills in the Haworth area in 1820.

owned a butcher's shop and, coincidentally, a Samuel Hartley was killed at the attack of Rawfold's Mill in Cleckheaton during the Luddite rebellions of 1812. In her later novel, *Shirley*, the name Hartley is revived and reimagined as the Antinomian weaver, Michael Hartley. Delirious with religion, drink and politics, he attempts to murder the hero of Charlotte's novel, Robert Moore.

Greenwood was another prominent family name in Haworth, so much so that to list their family history and divisions would be another chapter within itself. Therefore, it is likely that the James Greenwood Esqr of the manuscript is referring to the Greenwoods of Bridgehouse, the oldest and foremost manufacturing family in the village. The older James Greenwood lived between the years 1763 and 1824; upon his death he left the mill to the eldest and youngest of his brood, John (1784-1833) and James Jr (1793-1857). James Jr and family were practising Baptists and at the centre of the Dissenter disagreements of the 1830s. It makes sense therefore that Charlotte would choose him as another non-conformist target in her story.

Mr Robson may be a play on the name Roberson, a Reverend and friend of the Revd. Brontë who is said to have ridden up to a Luddite riot at Rawfold's Mill armed with a sword. Charlotte would later immortalise him as the militant Reverend Helstone in *Shirley*. Finally, Mr Sunderland, based on Abraham Sunderland, the Keighley organist who taught the Brontës music from late 1833 onwards, appears to be caught in the satirical crossfire. Charlotte finishes the manuscript with him being frightened into "temporary insanity".[8]

This psychological reference is, in itself, important, reinforcing Charlotte's early fascination and anxiety concerning the human mind, trauma, and temporary lapses in reality.[9] Think, for example, of the Angrian soldier, Henry Hastings. Charlotte chose him as the subject of her last novella, exploring his degeneration from national poet and soldier in the Angrian army, to alcoholic deserter whose "nerves were shaken" by the terrors of war. Think also of her fictitious version of Napoleon in *The Green Dwarf*, who, after admitting the horrifying reality of his actions, falls into a temporary state of catalepsy.[10] The latter tale, written in September of this same year, indicates that the topic of madness remained of interest to Charlotte throughout that year, and inspired her to expand her representations of fragile, unstable masculinity.

In one short manuscript Charlotte introduces us to a full array of characters, some recognisable, some not. What most have in common is that they are either Dissenters or hyperbolic, hysterical, somewhat comical characters that are in some way connected to the church. Some are familiar to us as future reincarnations – much of this manuscript prefigures some of the satire and critique in *Shirley*. Other

8   This would not be the last time we come across Sunderland in the juvenilia. In Charlotte's later Angrian tales, he is reimagined as Sudbury Figgs, friend of Zamorna's music master, Mr John Greenwood. This Greenwood is another contender for the manuscript's Greenwood influence: in real life he is the famous organist in Leeds.

9   Think also of the female characters of her later published works: Lucy Snowe and Bertha Mason. In *Villette*, Lucy suffers a severe temporary lapse in reality when left at the Pennsionnat Heger over a prolonged summer period, and wanders the streets in acute emotional distress. In *Jane Eyre*, Bertha, the insane wife of Mr Rochester, suffers her severe bouts of violent mental anguish in a cycle, perhaps, as feminist critics have argued, as a way of addressing women's bodily instability whilst menstruating.

10   Catalepsy is broadly defined as a form of seizure, where a person is immobilized, rigid, and in a trance-like state.

instances make us think of other juvenilia tales: either we think back to previous mini-plots, or recognise characters that will resurface in different forms in Charlotte and Branwell's later Angrian tales.

What this manuscript does contribute individually, however, is setting. By bringing her fantasy world home to Haworth, we have a clear vision of Charlotte engaging, if offensively, with her local community. We also realise that the siblings' world, built on the shores of an exotic African climate, is not very far away from their Yorkshire roots at all. More than ever, we can see how events and characters in their local community shape their stories, and realise that their kingdom was an imaginary landscape where the siblings could explore the political, religious and even local fabric of their childhood: it was not just an exercise in play and escapism, it was a platform for which they could understand and critique the world around them.

CHARLOTTE'S LUST FOR VIOLENCE

Charlotte Brontë's writings transgress nineteenth-century normative borders. Her famous works, such as *Jane Eyre* and *Villette*, have both been critiqued and celebrated for their treatment of sex, violence, madness, and vice. Think, for example, of the problematic Bertha Mason in *Jane Eyre*, who embodies all the negative characteristics that have the potential to turn a woman into something truly monstrous: she is angry, seductive, passionate, and primal. Even the main relationship in the text, between Jane and Rochester, has been read by some academics to be some form of sadomasochistic dialogue based on a master/servant relationship.[11]

Charlotte's published works were a tame outlet for her imagination; yet, even these writings agitated the anxieties of the British reading public. Currer Bell was, to many, a writer with dangerous, undisciplined and un-Christian values. Imagine, then, if that same

---

11   See, for example, Charles Bussbaum's *Understanding Pornographic Fiction* (2016), and Louisa Yates' essay 'Reader I [shagged/beat/whipped/f****d/rewrote] him in Amber Regis's and Deborah Wynne's *Charlotte Brontë: Legacies and Afterlives* (2017).

public had been exposed to her juvenilia. Within their private universe no Victorian social problem or taboo is off limits: off hand, these include seduction, mistresses, illegitimate children, homosocial relationships, alcoholism, violence, war – the list goes on.

This new manuscript only adds to the collection of juvenilia where Charlotte's uninhibited self spills unapologetically on to the page. Her merging of Glass Town and Haworth brings her playful, mischievous side to the surface. Yet within the short tale she provides us with a quantity of vice in the form of violence, alcoholism, and insanity. How does this fit in with the rest of her juvenilia – and what does it tell us about Charlotte's wild side?

Violence exists in many forms within the Brontë juvenilia. Branwell's war epics, such as *A Historical Narrative of Encroachment and Aggression* (1833-34), bring us no end of bloodshed and gore: heads are chopped off, bodies are burnt and hung, eyes are gouged out. This is not to say that violence is purely reserved for the soldiers of the saga. Charlotte transferred the horrors of combat into the domestic sphere, filling her country estates and domestic drawing rooms with the same hot-headed men that dealt blows on the battlefield.

One of her early violent tales specifically involves the hero of this newly discovered manuscript, Charles Wellesley. Charlotte wrote *A Day at Parry's Palace* (1830) when she was fourteen. The story opens with Charles visiting Parry's Land, one of the many provinces in the Glass Town saga. Here, he visits Captain Parry's Palace. Upon entering he is entertained by the occupants of the house. He is soon, however, left in the company of a child. After laughing at him, Charles was incensed:

> *having the poker, I struck him to the ground. The scream that he set up was tremendous, but it only increased my anger. I kicked him several times & dashed his head against the floor, hoping to stun him. This failed. He only roared the louder.*[12]

12 Christine Alexander, *Tales of Glass Town, Angria and Gondal* (2010), pp. 41-2.

This violent scene is graphic and shocking. What makes it more shocking is that the tale is written by a young girl, from the perspective of an adult male, with the violence directed toward a toddler. Charlotte, it is clear, was used to indulging in the darker side of her imagination. This encourages us to read the new manuscript as one in a series of Charlotte's unrestrained, raw juvenilia stories: Charlotte's explicit language and content was not unconventional. Like the child in Parry's Palace, people are dragged, beaten, and humiliated: there is some sort of sadistic enjoyment embedded latently within these lines.

Charlotte's lust for violence goes further than this, however. Regularly, throughout her early juvenilia tales she gratifies her fantasies for a specific type of violence: flogging. In *An Interesting Passage in the Lives of Some Eminent Men of the Present Time* (1830) a minor character, Bobadil, based on a character in Ben Jonson's Early Modern play *Every Man in His Humour* (1598), is served justice from the whip of Hume Badey, the Glass Town physician – and real life physician to the Duke of Wellington:

> *General Bobadill: May it please you, my lord, Sir Alexander Hume Badey has with the most consummate insolence horse-whipped me while in the discharge of my duty.*

> *Duke of Wellington: Well, it certainly does please me, Bobadill*[13]

There is a militant formality to this admission, yet there are also underlying sexual connotations in the dichotomy between whipping and pleasure. This is only emphasised by other manuscripts that show the Duke of Wellington – Charlotte's idol – and his son, the Duke of Zamorna – Charlotte's crush – repeating this same whipping/pleasure scenario. In *Military Conversations* (1829) the Duke of Wellington orders the drunken Alexander Hume Badey, the flogger of the previous manuscript, to be taken to the 'triangle', a frame

---

13 *EEW I* 1987, p. 185.

to which a soldier was bound in order to be flogged.

Additionally, the mingling of violence and sexuality is revealed through Zamorna's boxing name. Although, in the early nineteenth century, it was common for boxers to be branded with bawdy, pugilist names, such as Jem Belcher, Tom Tring, and Ikey Pig,[14] Charlotte calls her muscular champion a number of names that are easily classified as *double entendres*: The Swashing Swell, Young Wildblood, and the Handsome Spanker.

This manuscript is, again, another story in a long line of writings that address familiar, if somewhat risqué, themes. Mr John Hartley is publically flogged in the street, much like Bobadil or Hume Badey. This literary outlet for the punishment and humiliation of men is shocking, but somewhat falls in line with the fantasies and private, rebellious thoughts of a young girl going through puberty, who would have been especially exposed to the ideals and expectations of leading a godly way of life. What this example adds to this sexual narrative, however, is that Charlotte's fantasies were not just reserved for 'eminent', somewhat mythical, characters in her life, but also the very townspeople who she and her family interacted with on a daily basis.

THE VALUE OF THE DISCOVERY

The discovery of *A Visit to Haworth* is an important addition to the collective Brontë library. It holds two-fold significance in Brontë studies. First, it is a rare insight into Charlotte's relationship with the people of Haworth, and second, that it further consolidates Charlotte's interest and participation in the extreme, violent themes that run through her juvenilia and into her later published works. For the first time, her physical and mental homes – Haworth and Glass Town – meet, and through their meeting we are gifted an explosive insight into the darker, maturing elements of Charlotte's imagination.

---

14   These names were taking from popular pugilist periodicals of the day, such as *Bell's Life in London*.

FRAGMENTS OF GLASS

Sarah E. Maier

Boys, blood/lust and beauty
in Charlotte Brontë's juvenilia

To read the juvenilia of Charlotte Brontë is a surprise to those readers who are only aware of her novels; Byronic heroes locked in a battle for alpha-male supremacy, jealous brothers cynically evaluating the outcome, and loyal women of intelligence cast as pawns in the West African realm of Glass Town are, at the very least, unexpected in the energetic writings of her youth.

The recovery of her mother's Henry Kirke White volume, with its pasted in scraps of prose and poetry surrounded by stories of shipwreck, are important new findings in Brontë scholarship. This essay considers how Charlotte constructs and mobilises the masculinities she creates and inhabits through a variety of masculine personae to consider bloodlust, boys and beauty, as well as how she uses them in the new fragments of Glass Town.

Dr Sarah E. Maier is Professor of English & Comparative Literature. Sarah has published on J. M. Barrie, E. D'Arcy, G. Eliot, T. Hardy, J. K. Rowling, B. Stoker and others. For the bicentennials, she is ensconced in the work of the Brontës, but her other research interests include Louisa May Alcott, Marie Corelli, Neo-Victorianism, Madness, and Children's as well as Young Adult fictions. She has been appointed University Teaching Scholar.

There is one just now crossing—a lady. I will not write her name,
though I know it. No history is connected with her identity. She
is not one of the transcendently fair & inaccessibly sacred beings
whose fates are interwoven with the highest of the high …

Charlotte Brontë, *Roe Head Journal*

L ong before Currer Bell unmasked herself to reveal Charlotte
Brontë, she co-created the large-scale juvenilia of the Glass
Town and Angria sagas with her brother, Branwell. In the
West African stories, she assumes a male alter ego in the guise of the
author, Lord Charles Wellesley. He is an insightful observer of his
older brother, the Byronic Duke of Zamorna, a once-removed child
witness of the world's imaginary, and perceived, foibles and furies.

The scribblemania, or 'scriblomania', of the juvenilia that
exercises the Brontës' "creative power carried to the verge of insanity"
(Gaskell 1997 398), now has exciting additions to its narrative with
the newly-discovered fragmentary pieces by Charlotte Brontë – one
a short prose episode, one a draft of a poem – found pasted into her
mother, Maria Brontë's, copy of *The Remains of Henry Kirke White*
(1810). This volume of poetry by the well-known juvenile author,
Henry Kirke White, was published posthumously while he was being
lamented as a model for the "young poets who come after him,"
including the great Romantic writer, George Gordon, Lord Byron.[1]
An interesting synchronicity occurs between Charlotte's mother's
ownership of the book, her father's knowledge of the author from
his days at Cambridge, and her siblings' access to this book, edited
in two volumes by Robert Southey, later Poet Laureate, and published
in its fourth edition in 1810. In two new fragments from the Glass
Town saga – one of prose, one of poetry – Charlotte Brontë constructs
and mobilises the masculinities she creates to problematise gender
in her considerations of blood and lust, as well as how male success
is gained at the expense of the female and the beautiful.

1   According to John Barnard, *Remains* "was frequently reprinted. By 1818 there were ten editions" (390).

For some readers the idea of juvenilia – "literary or artistic works produced in the author's youth" – might strike the same out-dated negative notion as children's literature, that it may not be suitable for rigorous academic study because the ideas contained therein must necessarily be immature, un- or underdeveloped by the author. The important point is that the term "juvenilia" is not as stable as official dictionary definitions would suggest. As attitudes to childhood itself change, and as readers, students and editors discover the rich rewards in the field of literary juvenilia, the negative connotations of the term begin to slip from the control of canonical writers of the past. But this is a slow process, "especially since the definition has been based on the biographical criterion of age" according to Brontë scholar, Christine Alexander. Further, when the political or the social are "appropriated by the child-author [it] allows her to experience the adult world while at the same time challenging the ideologies it professes" and that is, in many ways, "achieved partly through the protection that marginalisation and difference allow".

The assumption that childhood is always an innocent, protected moment without adult concerns or considerations was a luxury not granted to the Brontë children. On April 21st 1816, the Reverend Patrick Brontë née Brunty of County Down, Ireland, and Maria Branwell of Penzance, Cornwall, welcomed a third daughter, Charlotte, after Maria and Elizabeth. Fourteen months later, Patrick Branwell joined the sisters, while Emily Jane and Anne brought the Brontë family to full fruition by 1820. The curacy had been given to their father the year before, and his sister-in-law, Elizabeth Branwell, joined the family to care for the siblings' terminally ill mother who succumbed to cancer eight months later.

These were not the final tragedies for the young family. The eldest girls were initially sent in succession to the Clergy Daughters' school at Cowan Bridge in Lancashire, but they were recalled when Maria, and then Elizabeth, were rushed home only to die shortly thereafter of consumption. Charlotte Brontë's youth was one of family losses, childhood confusion, and precocious understanding; there is a clear crisis between Charlotte's urgent need for expressing her knowledge while being agonisingly aware that she has, as yet, no voice.[2]

On March 12th 1829, in one of her first known writings, Charlotte Brontë explains the catalyst for the early beginnings of the Glass Town saga were, in fact, childhood toys given to her brother, Branwell, on June 5th 1826. The children's excitement is clear in her description:

> *Papa bought Branwell some soldiers from Leeds. When Papa came home it was night and we were in bed, so next morning Branwell came to our door with a box of soldiers. Emily and I jumped out of bed and I snatched up one and exclaimed, 'This is the Duke of Wellington! It shall be mine!' When I said this, Emily likewise took one and said it should be hers. When Anne came down she took one also. Mine was the prettiest of the whole and perfect in every part. Emily's was a grave-looking fellow. We called him 'Gravey'. Anne's was a queer little thing, very much like herself. He was called 'Waiting Boy'. Branwell chose 'Bonaparte'.*

Although the children variously appropriated their soldiers, it was the potential to create narratives and worlds for the little men that captured their imaginations. The Brontës' childhood plays developed into several literary narratives including origin stories, romantic tales, periodicals, catalogues, histories, speeches, advertisements, reviews, novellas, poems, and fragments. The first three plays, *Young Men* (June 1826), *Our Fellows* (July 1827) and *Islanders* (December 1827), form the basis for Charlotte's "world below". After the deaths of their elder sisters in 1825, Charlotte, Branwell, Emily and Anne began their literary play, and by 1829, they had set out as serious sibling writers – Charlotte with Branwell, and Emily with Anne – working in pairs to create the powerful worlds of Glass Town, Angria, and Gondal. The four small Brontës

---

2   Juliet McMaster's paradigm for the epistemology of the child (2005 52) fits this world of the Brontë children.

(aged ten, nine, eight and seven respectively) metamorphose to become the omniscient and powerful Genii (Talli, Branni, Emmi and Anni) of these West African adventures.

In contrast to their obsessively tiny writing and diminutive physical size of the "little books" they created, the scope and intricacies of these juvenile writings demonstrate that far from a standard childhood education of the time, these children had been immersed with their father's library into the wider worlds of literature and politics. Patrick Brontë encouraged his children to be informed on the political questions of the day, to have well-

Letter written by "UT". This refers to "Us Two", Charlotte and Branwell, who were jointly complaining against the tyranny of the four Chief Genii (the Brontë children) in their fantasy world of Glass Town. The letter is addressed to editor of the *Young Men's Magazine*.

considered opinions and to contribute to family discussions that often ended in rigorous debate. Aside from ongoing interest in the Bible, its teachings and its characters,[3] or world geographical study in Reverend J. Goldsmith's *A Grammar of Geography*, the Brontë family's reading included ancient to current texts, from Aesop's *Fables*, *Arabian Nights*, John Bunyan's *Pilgrim's Progress*, Homer's *Odyssey*, John Milton's *Paradise Lost*, and Virgil's *Aeneid*, to Sir Walter Scott's novels as well as the Romantic works of Lord Byron, Percy Bysshe Shelley, Robert Southey and William Wordsworth.

In addition, there is a connection to the new fragments found in the *Remains*; Byron was an admirer of Kirke White, a significant point given the young Brontë family's admiration of Byron and his influence on their sagas. According to biographer Claire Harman:

> *Patrick Brontë seems to have made no attempt to keep Byron away from his children, and the results were very marked. Charlotte is so familiar with the scandalous atheist's works by the age of ten that she quotes them freely in her own stories and both she and Branwell came to admire him – for his style, bravado, wit and sensual excesses.*

These influences pervade the Glass Town tales. There is a precocious mixing of real and imagined characters with intellectual commentaries as well as warmongering conflicts, all of which lead to authorial empowerment in their narrative play. Family discussions of Napoleon Bonaparte, the Duke of Wellington and the many debates found in *Blackwood's Edinburgh Magazine* or *Fraser's Magazine* find their way, amongst others, to intermingle with the children's own developing prose. Without question, the writing, and music, of the Romantics had a strong place in their minds and hearts.[4] Byron, John Keats, and Shelley all read Kirke White; indeed,

---

3 Christine Alexander, editor of the juvenilia, reminds us of the importance of Biblical allusion in Charlotte Brontë's work because it was "a fertile source of imagery and inspiration for the young author. The drama and colour of the Old Testament and the prophetic visions of the New Testament appealed especially to Charlotte's pictorial imagination. The world of the genii owes as much to the Book of Revelation as it does to the *Arabian Nights* and the *Tales of the Genii*." (1983 241).

4 Aside from the Brontë's reading(s) of the Romantic poets and essayists, Emily Brontë had a preference for the music of the contemporary period, including playing the work of Ludwig von Beethoven.

as young writers, they saw him as a "paradigm of all that youth might achieve", in much the same way as Thomas Chatterton who was held up for his juvenile writings that ended prematurely with his suicide at age seventeen.

The proximity of the Kirke White volume in their mother's belongings, along with the knowledge that he was appreciated by the Romantic poets whom they admired, may very well have encouraged the Brontë children to read Kirke White's work thereby intangibly influencing their own early works. Writers in the juvenile tradition often "hail others like them to seize for themselves the ontology of juvenility – to speak the subject position that they inhabit but that older writers can misconstrue, appropriate, limit, or deny". Further, it is better – in opposition to previous definitions that classify juvenilia by age – to consider that what defines a juvenile writer is not age to a finite date, but rather how the author presents themselves and how their texts are received. No one would argue that the Brontë children were unaware of the literary world they privately sought to enter.

Charlotte was keenly aware of the difficulties that confronted her as a child, a girl, and a sibling writer. While Kirke White writes with pride in *Remains* that "the Author is very conscious that [these are] the juvenile efforts of a youth" (II 5), Charlotte dismisses her own early efforts. She is eager to participate in the literary sphere but is fully aware of the limitations imposed on her by her sex and her age. When she wrote to Southey for encouragement – hoping for much as he gave to Kirke White – he, instead, rebuffed her ambition by return letter of March 23rd 1837, with his opinion that "there is a danger of which I would with all kindness and earnestness warn you. The day-dreams in which you habitually indulge are likely to induce a distempered state of mind … Literature cannot be the business of a woman's life, & it ought not to be". His indifference to her writing confronts Charlotte with an early reminder of the gendered spheres of life but gives the readers some understanding

Portrait by Charlotte, said to be of her lifelong friend, Ellen Nussey.

of the pseudonymous masks she would choose to wear in order to speak without reserve. She realised that she must create a divide between "her life as Currer Bell, the author; [and] her life as Charlotte Brontë, the woman" as Gaskell saw her.[5]

In one example of the self-censorship expected of a young woman, she explains in a letter dated September 5th 1832 to her lifelong friend and correspondent, Ellen Nussey, that she does not write to her of political intrigue because "I believe you would not find much to interest you in a political discussion". Politics aside, the two young women had enlightening exchanges about literature that demonstrated Charlotte's expansive knowledge. In response to Ellen Nussey's request for a reading list, she replies: "[if] you like poetry let it be first rate, Milton, Shakespeare, Thomson, Goldsmith Pope (if you will though I don't admire him) Scott, Byron, Camp[b]ell, Wordsworth and Southey. Now Ellen don't be startled at the names of Shakespeare, and Byron" but there are also suggestions for her friend to omit "Don Juan, perhaps the Cain of Byron though the latter is a magnificent Poem and read the rest fearlessly" including "Scott's sweet, wild,

5   For a discussion of her post-juvenile writing pseudonym, see Maier 2017.

romantic Poetry" but for fiction, "read Scott alone all novels after his are worthless". The list continues with authors and titles from history, biography, natural history as well as divinity. In another letter on New Year's Day, January 1st 1833, Charlotte's attention is arrested by Sir Walter Scott's *Kenilworth* (1821) because it

> *... is certainly a splendid production more resembling a Romance than a Novel [...] I was exceedingly amused at the characteristic and naïve manner in which you expressed your detestation of Varney's character [...] he is certainly the personification of consummate villainy and in the delineation of his dark and profoundly artful mind Scott exhibits a wonderful knowledge of human nature as well as surprising skill in embodying his perceptions so as to enable others to become participators in that knowledge.*

Elizabeth Gaskell, in her *The Life of Charlotte Brontë* (1857), paints a picture of the odd little packet of papers that are "almost impossible to decipher" and if readable – even literally due to their size – are intelligible only to "the bright little minds" who wrote them because "they are the wildest & most incoherent" narratives. To the young siblings, they are a "vision's spell" woven into a "web".

In a moment of early prescience, Charlotte admits that all "our plays are very strange ones. Their nature I need not write on paper for I think I shall always remember them". Written mostly between the ages of fourteen and twenty-four, even before she completes the first drafts of *The Professor*, her juvenilia prove that Charlotte sought to explore literary genres outside of the usual limits imposed on young women of society. Charlotte recognises her difference in her desire to know; indeed, she warns her friend Ellen Nussey, "don't deceive yourself by imagining that I have a bit of real goodness about me". She admits:

> *I am not like you. If you knew my thoughts; the dreams that absorb me; and the fiery imagination that at times eats me up and makes*

The stories written by the Brontë children reveal their unique vision of a fantasy world. The coin indicates the size of the 'little books'.

me feel Society as it is, wretchedly insipid. You would pity and I dare say despise me [because] when I stoop down to drink of the pure waters they fly from my lips as if I were Tantalus.[6]

Like Tantalus, Charlotte continually thirsts after something more. The one sibling who was most able to understand Charlotte was, according to her, Branwell. Over time, the intellectual bond between the then two eldest siblings intensified; once apart from him and back at Roe Head, she wrote to him on May 17th 1832:

I had begun to think that I had lost all the interest which I used formerly to take in politics but the extreme pleasure I felt at the

6   Tantalus is the son of Zeus who is cursed with insatiable thirst; every time he tries to drink from the pool in which he stands under a fruit tree, the water is always out of reach.

news [of the Reform Bill and various activities] convinced me that
I have not as yet lost all my penchant for politics.

Simultaneously, she confesses "to you I find the most to say" and is disoriented when he is absent. In her *Roe Head Journal* on August 11th 1836, she observed that outside of her home environment that includes intense sibling interaction, she is a wreck because

All this day I have been in a dream, half miserable & half ecstatic: miserable because I could not follow it out uninterruptedly; ecstatic because it shewed almost in the vivid light of reality the ongoings of the infernal world [that] came on me, rushing impetuously, all the mighty phantasm that we had conjured from nothing to a system strong as some religious creed. I felt as if I could have written gloriously—I longed to write.

In one instance, in spite of her ability to be an adaptable collaborator to sudden, rapid changes introduced by Branwell, Charlotte's anxiety that her brother's narrative trajectory has betrayed her main female character is overwhelming:

Is she dead? Is she buried? Is she alone in the cold earth on this dreary night? I hope she's alive still, partly because I can't abide to think how hopelessly and cheerlessly she must have died, and partly because her removal, if it has taken place, must have been to Northangerland like the quenching of the last spark that averted utter darkness.

In spite of the appeal to see her writing as spiritual, her description of her own practice is fraught with language of addiction when, after a difficult day of teaching girls she loathes, Charlotte admits: *"Delicious was the sensation I experienced as I laid down"* so the *"toil of the day, succeeded by this moment of divine leisure, had acted on me like opium & was coiling about me a disturbed but fascinating spell, such as I never felt before. What I imagined grew morbidly vivid"*.

Self-portrait of Branwell: Branwell was Charlotte's closest collaborator but their alliance ended as he became increasingly self-destructive.

A page from the *Roe Head Journal*, starting with the words: "All this day I have been in a dream". Charlotte found it almost impossible to reconcile her everyday life with the imaginings of her fantasy world.

Upon her return to Roe Head, Charlotte even hallucinates her creations; she confesses in her journal: "I hear them speak…I see distinctly their figures—and though alone, I experience all the feelings of one admitted for the first time into a grand circle of classic beings…transcendently fair and accessible sacred being". For Charlotte, to be away from her "world below," the fictional Glass Town where she was fully herself, was to take away her lifeblood.

BOYS BECOME MEN

Unlike at Roe Head where mediocrity consumed energy, at home Charlotte's ideas coalesced "to form a defined picture". This is in the context of the fierce competition, but mutual dependence upon her brother, for the saga's ongoing developments of war and politics to which she provides the personae of its people. Their collaboration sets the foundation for when the toy soldiers of childhood play have, now in Glass Town/Verdopolis, grown from boys to men.

The Duke of Wellington retains dominion over his sons, Arthur and Charles, but only to a point. In a prefiguring of Charlotte's adult use of 'Currer Bell', the juvenilia sees her perform as Lord Charles Wellesley, Charles Tree, and later as the renamed Wellesley, now Charles Townshend. The sublimation of the child author into male narrator(s) and fictional persona(s), Wellesley – as one of her male pseudonyms within the sagas – usually acts the disempowered, informant observer, while his brother Arthur, the Marquis of Douro (later Duke of Zamorna, King of Angria and Emperor Adrian) indulges in womanising, sexual escapades, serial marriage, nation building, and political battle, particularly with and against Alexander Percy (Rogue, later Duke of Northangerland and Lord Elrington).

A significant element of the early work is the multiplicity of the many male voices employed by both Branwell and Charlotte. Charlotte's "assumption of various masks allows her to argue as much with her own polyphonic voices" (Alexander 2010 xxi) as with those of Branwell, and to analyse, as well as assume, literary authority of and in the narratives. Working from various positional points of view, Charlotte indulges in the freedom of male play in the realms of boyhood, blood relations, lustful desire and captured beauty.

The two new fragments are exciting additions to the saga and our understanding of two singular male characters, and the woman between them. The prose fragment gives us a glimpse into the direction of development of one brother, Charles, and

Arthur, Marquis of Douro, drawn by Charlotte, 1833.

the poetry piece gives us a new view of the other brother, Arthur. In the externalised Haworth episode, Charles goes from passive and sarcastic to obnoxious and physical. In the internalised poetic musing of Arthur, he changes from a man of war to a man longing for a recommitment to his love. Each case, once considered within the larger context of the appropriate point of the Glass Town narrative, represents a new insight into each male character.

The tales begin much like a boy's adventure story with *the Twelve Adventurers and Tales of the Islanders* on a voyage of discovery to seek out and mark further territory for the Empire in which they immediately kill natives, ransom a Chief, and accept a proposition of "peace from their King [...] on terms the most advantageous to

ourselves". The creation of the pillars of their transplanted society
– the Hall of Justice, the Grand Inn, the Great Tower, and the
fortifications of war – are completed in the capital with the magic of
the Genii. In a moment of quiet observation, Captain Bud describes:

> *2 young men, or rather boys, apparently of about 17 or 18 years of*
> *age. They were tall, slender, remarkably handsome, and were so*
> *much alike that it would have been difficult to distinguish the one*
> *from the other, were it not for a shade of thought which occasionally*
> *passed over the features of the elder; and his fine way hair was also*
> *a little darker than that of the other, whose merry smile, which now*
> *and then lighted up his handsome face, and the gaiety with which*
> *he would sometimes toss aside his own light, curly hair and the*
> *playful manner in which he spoke to his brother when he observed*
> *the shade of thought come across his fine features, all betokened*
> *a more gay disposition than that which belonged to the elder.*

Identified as Arthur and Charles, the two boys will grow into men
during the sagas. Here their prestige is established by the setting
of this encounter under a nine-hundred foot high "round dome of
white agate, sparkling with stars of gold and rich ornaments of purple
sapphire" in the Palace of Waterloo that is the residence of their
father, the heroic Duke of Wellington.

As in Charlotte's own society, the men embroil themselves in
issues of patriarchal entitlements and expansion, both politically
and personally. The "mightiest of the armies" protect the "City of
Might (as the Glass Town is called by that admirable novelist Captain
Tree)" and the eminent men who live therein. In 'Chapter the 2' of
the December 1829 periodical of the juvenilia, Charlotte pauses to
colour at length the personalities of many men including the Duke
of Wellington who "is without dispute [. . .] decisive, calm, courageous,
and noble-minded" while he remains the new nation's hero. There
are descriptions of men with villainous possibilities initially crafted
by Branwell to stand against Charlotte's virtuous man. Rogue is

a handsome counterpart, with "something very startling in his fierce, grey eyes and formidable forehead. His manner is rather polished and gentlemanly, but his mind is deceitful, bloody, and cruel"; in addition, his agile ability to resort to trickery is suggested when he plays cards with skill at the gaming table while being excessively vain of his talents. Rogue, Young Man Naughty, and Pigtail – characters invented by Branwell – are all early capable foils to the potential brilliance of the Wellesley line.

The Wellesley boys become eminent men styled Marquis of Douro and Lord Charles Wellesley. Douro, now aged twenty-two, "resembles his noble mother" in his height, slender shape, and Roman nose, but in his large eyes and dark auburn glossy hair, he resembles the father; most importantly, his character "resembles the Duchess's, mild and human but very courageous, grateful for any favour that is done and ready to forgive injuries, kind to others and disinterested in himself".

Described much like a visionary Romantic poet, Captain Tree continues to claim the elder young man's "mind is of the highest order, elegant and cultivated. His genius is lofty and soaring […] with the meditations of a lonely traveler in the wilderness or the mournful song of a solitary exile are the themes in which he most delights and which he chiefly indulges in". Captain Tree admires the nineteen-year old younger sibling as "striking and handsome. His eye is full of life and vigour" with light blonde ringlets, animated expression, and charming. A great deal is made of Lord Charles's "lively, gay and elegant" appearance that matches his "sharp and piercing" wit that "he often lets […] play harmlessly round his opponent, then strikes him fiercely to the heart", likely because his "imagination is exceedingly vivid, as the graphic delineation of nature and character is" as a man of genius.

The two men are now set up in contradiction, with Douro like the "soft reverberations of an Aeolian harp which […] raise the soul to a pitch of wild sublimity or lead it to mournful and solemn thought" juxtaposed with how, after you read a book by Lord Charles, "you feel light and gay and merry, as if you could read on air". The eldest son is extremely passionate but with *gravitas*, while the younger man is easily dismissed as non-threatening, a trait that will serve Lord Charles well as he narrates his brother's developing lust for blood and beauty. The two boys grow to men, both fierce competitors who show themselves in the new fragments for who, perhaps, they each would rather be.

BLOOD/LUST AND MANHOOD

In what might be our last fragment of new material of the Glass Town tales, Charlotte tells of Lord Charles bringing his entourage to Haworth, an episode unseen in any previous juvenilia. Like the other tales, this is a fragmented event in the loosely woven web of narratives; these sketches or scenes, are not neat and tidy. There is always a sense of the incomplete, a prefiguring of the fragility of both the Glass Town narrative as Charlotte grows older and the delicate nature of the balance between male egos as Charles becomes socially hostile in the prose, and Zamorna's long-ignored poetic understanding yearns for something more than war.

At this point, the narrative voice of Lord Charles is derisive, degenerate, and disconcerting in tales like another juvenile piece *Stancliffe's Hotel* (1838/39).[7] Charlotte Brontë casts a gossipy conversation between two minor characters, Bravey and Sydney, to reveal the extreme changes in the Wellesley men. Sydney asks if there is any likeness between this "small imp of a brother" and Zamorna, to which Bravey responds "Not the least. Lord Charles is a little vile, ugly, lying, meddling, messing, despicable dirty ape, who delights in slandering all good and great men and in consorting with all wicked and mean ones" while Zamorna is to "the objects of his

---

7   Heather Glen (2006) dates the five tales, *Mina Laury*, *Stancliffe's Hotel*, *The Duke of Zamorna*, *Henry Hastings* and *Caroline Vernon*, between January 1838 and December 1839, while Charlotte Brontë definitively dates *Mina Laury* as 17 January 1838 at Haworth (Brontës 220) which implies that *Stancliffe's Hotel* followed that date.

regard he's an angel, but to those of his hatred, a very Lucifer".
It is now clear that Lord Charles' observations are not objective or
without opinion or emotion, sometimes ranging toward the homicidal;
he even admits in the preface to Albion and Marina that "I have
written this tale out of malignity for the injuries that have lately
been offered to me".

This newly-discovered fragment is two pages, written in large
cursive long hand of sepia ink, and focusing on Lord Charles
Wellesley; it is self-dated as "June 1833" and there is enough
similarity with her writings of that time or shortly thereafter to see
it fit contextually in Charlotte Brontë's juvenile writing. This fragment
brings together the cynicism of earlier prose pieces with the language
to describe men at their worst. Much has changed about Lord
Charles since the descriptions of him from December of 1829. The
second-born son, unable to wield patriarchal power, he is self-exiled
and self-renamed; Charles Townshend Esqr by choice, he no longer
performs the part of a scion of the Wellesley family name, and he
no longer plays the part of a detached observer of his brother whom
he has left behind. The privileges of the first-born son have been
given to Zamorna; the lust for a life lived, or the diminished power
over inferiors, is now what is left to Townshend who becomes
a subjective participant in social debauchery and violence.

Now seemingly without a moral compass, he lowers himself to
a life of thievery, disruption and sadistic pleasure; observed by an
alternate male narrator who describes for the reader the degenerate
behaviour of Townshend, as well as his companion, "a little old man
of most suspicious aspect whom he called Mr Robert Thing." The two
men act as "brothers" and "passed themselves off for two ministers"
when they arrive at the "Black Bull". At the "Black Bull", not
coincidentally the site of Branwell's own increasingly bad behaviour,
Townshend's "manners and appearance [are] not such as are often
seen in a country village" nor is his behaviour amongst a "company
of the very riff raff of the place." He "delight[s] to fill [these men] with

as much drink as they could hold" then, to sit by to "witness and sometimes participate in the quarrels which arose out of their inebriety," the entertained catalyst and sometimes accomplice in their degeneracy. The village of Haworth is disrupted from its contained sorrows through the corruption of its men by excessive drink.

In a series of outrageous public acts, Townshend and Thing "embezzle the proceeds of the Quarterly Collection" and then attack with the objective to humiliate various churchmen. The "Revd John Winterbottom [is] "dragged from his bed [and] drawn by the heels from one end of the village to the other", while another, John Foster, is accosted then "dunked in a horse pond" while Mr Robson is half hung, and they "publicly flogged Mr John Hartley, tripped up the feet of James Greenwood Esqr [and] "frightened Mr Sunderland […] into temporary insanity." Townshend and his partner in crime, "after the commission of all these enormities made a moonlight flitting from the Black Bull without paying a sliver of his reckoning."

Both humorous and contemptible in its scope – while satirical in its tone – perhaps what is more startling is that the men of the prose piece are both fictional characters and factual persons. Charlotte Brontë's juvenile writings are full of portraits of her siblings and other people with whom she comes into contact. That said, they are usually given anonymity through renaming – even the character "Robert Thing" is a rewriting of Branwell's Glass Town character, "Robert Patrick King," one of his veiled narrators who act as his voice in the saga. Here, Robert Thing is twice-removed from the subject of scorn but is clearly a follower of the stronger man, Townshend.

While it is not altogether unusual for the Brontës to mock the clergy in the Angria stories, it is usually in a more removed manner, not as named individuals. For this fragment, the men of the clergy described appear as themselves. The *Reverend John Winterbotham* was a Baptist minister who once stood in opposition to Patrick Brontë, but also acted as one of three secretaries to him in the Temperance Society of Haworth, then later led the West Lane Baptist Chapel. *Mr. Robson* may be a London citizen, William Robson, who was responsible for the award given to Patrick at Cambridge, or possibly a Wesleyan minister in Whitby, Yorkshire. *James Greenwood* was the owner of Bridgehouse Mills, a Baptist and a leader of the Dissenters at Hall Green Baptist Chapel. *Mr. Abraham Stansfield Sunderland* was the Brontë children's music teacher and, indeed, the Keighley organist who, according to Patrick Brontë's letter of September 17th 1833, "give[s] his services gratis" when the new organ opened with a performance of Handel's *Messiah*. It is interesting that one of these real life persons, Mr. Sunderland, does appear as the character Mr. Sudbury Figgs in Glass Town narratives, so it seems irregular that he exists here in a doubling of his own previous characterisation. In each case, Townshend brings them away from the spiritual or ephemeral into the dirt or degradation of the physical realm, perhaps as a reminder they need to engage with the immediate realm of concerns in Haworth.

The irony is, of course, that this episode containing such comments on the ineffectiveness of the religious men on the debauchery of the interlopers, and their followers, is found in Kirke White's book in the hands of two successive men: Patrick Brontë, and then Arthur Bell Nicholls (Patrick's curate who later married Charlotte). The inscription of the elder Brontë demonstrates his admiration for Kirke White:

> *Hic Erat Liber, Uxoris mea charissimae, et servatus fuit ab undis — Igitur, semper servandus. — P.B.*

> *I had the honour of being acquainted at the University, with the subject of this memoir, and have every reason to think that the praise bestowed upon him, whether it respected him his genius or piety, — was well merited — P. Brontë*

Nicholls' own note has been pasted in as well:

The Parsonage,
Haworth.

Rev. & Dear Sir,

      On behalf of Mr Brontë &
myself I thank you sincerely for the sympathy expressed in your
note for us under our recent bereavement– The affliction is indeed
a heavy one, but we Endeavor to see in it the hand of our Heavenly
Father, "who does not willingly afflict the children of men," & console
ourselves by the reflection that our loss is her gain—
Again thanking you for your kindness

      I am Rev. & Dr Sir
      Yrs faithfully,
      A. B. Nicholls

The Biblical reference to Lamentations 3:33, "For he doth not afflict willingly nor grieve the children of men" (KJV) speaks to the fragment, not on purpose but unwittingly. The damage done to the men of Haworth by Townshend and Thing is, absolutely, inflicted by men through their individual will whereas God would not harm his children willingly. Here, in this episode, Charlotte's graphic demonstration of the cruel, harmful ways of men contrasts with the lofty readings of man found in the Bible, might also be an insight gleaned through the work of her father as he tends to his parish: less harm is heavenly sent than is cast by humans unto others.

To understand that both Maria and particularly Patrick Brontë held the author in esteem may explain why the fragments were placed in the book. The fact that, as leaders of the Church, either Brontë or Nicholls would have placed such a cynical outlook on the clergy within a valued Romantic text reminds us of the self-knowing laughter of Nicholls upon reading *Shirley* (1849) or from *Jane Eyre*, perhaps when Rochester reminds Jane that St. John Rivers is "a sort of raw curate, half strangled with his white neckcloth, and stilted up on his thick-soled high-lows".

BEAUTY BETWEEN MEN

To understand the importance of the new poetic fragment, we must remember that throughout the many narratives of the juvenile *oeuvre*, Charlotte takes the elder son, Arthur Wellesley, on a journey through the challenges of all the social complexities of his personal development, a kind of intense *bildungsroman*. Several critics believe that, early on in the tales, Charles Wellesley is Charlotte's observer of the increasing bloodlust of his brother. Bound by blood, but envious of the Duke of Zamorna's unchecked pursuit of pleasure, Wellesley/Townshend has now fallen to match his brother. In this newly discovered episode, amongst others perhaps lost and those preserved, Charlotte explores the fragility of male masks that conform to conventional behaviour, the difficulty of expectations of patriarchal roles placed on Charles and Arthur and the consequences of defiant rampant masculinity. When challenged by an equally strong personality, especially when the two men are locked into a duel of love and hate for each other, it is a woman who is sacrificed.

From Zamorna's early status as a young Romantic writer to his various titles that fuel his sense of entitlement, he grows into a complex Byronic figure who is sensual, charismatic and sadistic with "lofty heroic stature and free, bold, chivalric bearing" who now often has "a fiendish glitter" in his eyes that warn of a "strange madness!" in his mind. The earlier beauty, poetic temperament, and "effeminate delicacy" of the Duke now acts as a dissembling mask where "the eye-lids & long fringes partly concealed the sweet expression of vindictiveness lurking beneath". Shortness of temper is no longer assuaged by social convention. Once the "demon of Zamorna's nature [is] completely roused" in his transformative behaviour, he "Growl[s] out his words in a deep & hoarse tone almost like the smothered roar of a lion" as he creates a "spectacle of fierce manslaughter amid scenes of domestic peace" then in a deliberate act of civility, calmly rebuttons his gentlemanly surtout and dons his gloves.

The one man who matches the intangibility of the Marquis of Douro (later Zamorna) is the Duke of Northangerland (later Lord Elrington), with his blue frock coat, "white inexpungnables & a stiff black stock" who resembles that "angelic existence called a military man". He, too, becomes a Byronic figure under the intense, ambiguous gaze of Zamorna who sees "the great, vile, splendid, hateful, fiendish, angelic, black, bright, abominable, blessed scoundrel, that Northangerland, that illustriously infamous relative of mine, whom I abhor yet admire, detest and yet love, that bundle of contradictions and yet that horribly consistent whole".

This contradiction in both men – between the holy and the mighty, the artistic and the destroyer – confuses the "idea as to whether he is a god of perfection or a demon of defects [. . .] He is himself—a kind of abstract isolated being". Northangerland is known to be "filled [...] with the most restless contempt and hatred of mankind". The intensity of masculine competition run amok overwhelms their lives, including their relationships with their male children, and is only balanced by their entanglement with each other. In fact, the only check on the now Duke of Zamorna's power is the intensity of this male-male bond played out through a rivalry that is both homoerotic and homosocial. It is a relationship where the two men are charismatically drawn to each other, but immediately see each other as rivals. Their relationship – sometimes one of companionship, other times one of intense enmity – controls the fate of Glass Town. Their complex feelings for each other are further complicated by Branwell's creation of Northangerland's legitimate daughter, Mary Percy, as recounted in *The Politics of Verdopolis* by Captain John Flower, MP.[8]

Into this land of male-male competition that leads contextually to the poetic fragment, one woman is the connection between the two powerful men; Mary is Northangerland's daughter by his long dead, but greatly missed, first wife, Mary Henrietta Percy. His daughter

8   Captain John Flower, MP, is one of Branwell Brontë's pseudonyms. This first account of Mary occurs in Chapter One when she cries out to her father (Brontës 344) when he returns from visiting his wife, Mary Henrietta Percy's grave.

mary I stood thou didst not know that I was nigh
Thou didst not know my gaze was fixed on thee
I stood apart & watched thee gliding by
In all thy calm unconscious majesty
And drew apart under my spirit waking dreams
Through the bright mazes of that castled throng
With step that ~~took place~~ in spotless to dit with
Robes gems & masques & tossing plumes among
Around the light & ~~brilliant~~ the gladsome mirth
And though mine own Titania ! still as heaven
When not a cloud ~~but~~ floats in its fields of blue
When not a breath of ~~a~~ summer wind is given
Sighing the azure campaign ~~faint~~ softly through ~~one fell~~
Yes then I saw thee ~~pretty~~ ~~our~~ upon me ~~one soul~~
A dream that bore my spirit far away
I walked in thought through shadowed glade & dell
I left the day-light ~~sun~~ through foliage play
And thou wert there clothed in thy tunic green
The coronal of flowers ~~around~~ thy ~~brow~~ curls
The lily wand the bright zone sparkling sheen
& the long lucid chain of orient pearls
~~Of~~ ~~Isle of faerie~~
Methought 'twas night & I remembered well
As stars rose & ~~illumined~~ me ~~by me~~
Of many a sweet ~~wild~~ tale of Faerie
Of ~~many~~ dead in lonely greenwood tree
Titania left by her loved elfin King
And long by dell & hilly haunted glade
Tearless yet joyless ~~sadly~~ wandering
Seeking the dimmest path the thickest shade
Or else within her placid bower sleeping
~~Moonlight & dew~~ ~~her brow distilled~~
curtained with tendrils of the eglantine
Deserted Orchis & vetch, a spicy musk-rose creeping
To join their blossoms with the sweet woodbine
And for the fairy queen a veil to twine
Moonlight ~~the wild~~ ~~silver~~ around about her gleaming
through the young elms that made her canopy
And tears yes ~~from~~ her closed eye-lids streaming
Called forth by dreams that of her lost love be

The poetic fragment written by Charlotte.

Transcript of the poetic fragment

Mary ~~I stood~~ thou didst not know that I was nigh

Thou didst not know my gaze was fixed on thee

I stood apart & watched thee gliding by

In all thy calm unconscious majesty

~~And dreams make o'er my spirit, waking dreams~~

Through the bright mazes of that festal throng

With step that ~~woke scarce echo as it fell~~ fell like snow-flake to the earth

Robes gems & masques & tossing plumes among

Around thee light & ~~laughter~~ joy & gladsome mirth

And thou mine own Titania! still as heaven

When not a cloud floats in its fields of blue

When not a breath of summer wind is given

Sighing the azure campaign ~~faint~~ softly through

Yes then I saw thee & upon me ~~stole came~~ fell

A dream that bore my spirit far away

I walked in thought through shadowed glade & dell

I felt the day-light airs through foliage play

And thou wert there clothed in thy tunic green

The coronal of flowers ~~around~~ amid thy ~~brow~~ curls

The lily-wand, the bright zone sparkling sheen

& the long lucid chain of orient pearls

Of many & sweet sad tale of faiërie

Methought 'twas night & I remembered me

As stars rose & glimmered one by one

Of many a sweet wild tale of faerie

Of many a deed in lonely greenwood done

Titania left by her loved elfin King

And long by dell & hill & haunted glade

Tearless yet joyless sadly wandering

Seeking the dimmest path, the thickest shade

Or else within her placid bower sleeping

Moonlight & dew upon her brow distilled

Curtained with tendrils of the eglantine

Rose bud Orchis & vetch, & spicy musk-rose creeping

To join their blossoms with the sweet woodbine

And for the fairy queen a veil to twine

Moonlight like silver on & dew all round about her gleaming

Through the young elms that made her canopy

And tears alas from her closed eye-lids streaming

Called forth by dreams that of her lost love be

is, in the saga, an idealised child of the outdoors who, with an "unsophisticated custom" arises early "to walk through the park and up the sequestered lanes of this pastoral region" with her deer hound; idyllic but not necessarily ideal, a "large hat shaded the sun from her face and well set off her brown hair, expressive eyes and sunny smile" with which she "secure[s] the favour of the surrounding" rough, Irish like gentry with "her fairy shape, gentle voice and perfect cheerfulness". To keep pace with Branwell's changes, Charlotte Brontë has Zamorna's second wife, Marian, die of neglect in order to allow for his marriage to the romanticised Mary, and to enable the two dynasties to create a political coalition for mutual benefit.

Mary's entry into fashionable society sees her mask her Romanticism with "a different character" so she will be "looked up to, paid deference to, invited as the queen of their parties, and considered the standard of taste for the youth of the city" even though the *demi-monde's* "attentions were in vain". Mary tells Charles that, contrary to Zamorna's philandering ways, her husband "knows I am better than all my rivals and he loves me ten times more". Her ongoing and fierce loyalty is to her father, "he to whom she looked up with mingled fear, affection and awe". Amongst the women of society, Mary stands by her father "with a silent observant glance at the company round" but once they cast dispersions, her "eyes lighted up with all the fire of her father's. War and bloodshed might have been the consequence". The fated first meeting between Charlotte's passionate, well-experienced man and Branwell's young fairy woman solidifies the future entanglement of the two men when Northangerland introduces them.

Before even meeting him, Miss Percy had "read this young nobleman's glorious works until he himself, though she had never seen him, [was] fixed as firmly in her mind as her own father". Captain Flower details how her "admiration of him was unbounded, and being quite unsophisticated and unused to disguise her feelings, kindly or unkindly, she warmly took his offered hand and, with lighted eye and enthusiastic smile was, ere three minutes, firmly acquainted with him" while Zamorna "admired her enthusiasm, language and appearance" amongst the men. If she had been given the temperament of her father or empowered to speak, then she would have struck out, but she is long "practised in this kind of silent vigilance [. . .] when to speak & when to be silent"; indeed, it is Mary's passive deference and submission to the two leaders' combined masculinity that leads to her sacrificial exile, the wounding blow to his enemy, enacted by Zamorna.

Charlotte makes clear the cost of male play on others who surround the men, pointing out that they "never reflect that the relatives, the wives & daughters of those men, buried out of our sight amidst the seraglio existence of palaces, hear the same reports that we hear & feel as storms what we consider but slight clouds, & as arrow-heads what seem to us only snow-flakes". Mary knows she is a pawn who desires that her husband "would think of me more as a woman [. . .] & less as a bodiless link between himself & my terrible father" but she rages against her position: "I have a great stake in the Royal game now playing. If Northangerland & Zamorna make me the link between them, must not I who have a separate existence, urge my separate claims, and still try to work for myself an even path in this vale of tears through which we are all travelling?". Mary knows herself to be Beauty sacrificed in a game of male play.

Zamorna's strategic use of Mary does not negate his awareness of her pain. In the poem *Zamorna's Exile* (1836), he sees her in his mind's eye where "Her marble forehead, with the haloing hair/ Sunnily clustering round it" and how "dark care [...] has gloomed there of late".[9] Charlotte has Zamorna admit that women are the stronger sex because it is in the "ardour of our women's souls and spirits/That nought on earth such fire divine inherits" while he also knows Mary "said she'd die for me; and now she's keeping/Her word" as she exists in "aching pain" he wishes to ease. In spite of the pain

9 "Zamorna's Exile" in two cantos is also referred to by some critics as the poem "And when you left me."

it will cause to Mary and to himself, he declares his vengeance with "I've pledged my faith/I'll break the father's heart by Mary's death". He makes his intention clear to Mary with "I swore that if your father drew/His hand from mind, I'd give him back his gift" of pain to see that his "part in the great game is also played". In her role as a woman of insignificant significance, and in spite of his love for Mary, Zamorna, her "life for bloody vengeance sold" – sends his "dazzling lily" away with "It is his fault – I love you".

The new poetic fragment found in the Kirke White volume, "Mary thou didst not know that I was nigh," is a contemplation of Mary's importance to the man, not the mythic persona, who rules Glass Town. The poem contains iambic pentameter with alternate rhymes to a total of seventy-two lines on two pages of miniscule printing in pencil that is seemingly under active revision or has been heavily revised by Charlotte. The material content places the piece as possibly contemporaneous with *Zamorna's Exile* (1836) wherein he contemplates what he has done in the past, while in this fragment, it is clear that Zamorna watches Mary in a present, active manner without her knowledge or consent. It is not accidental that this expression of his poignancy of desire and defeat is poetic. In the context of the Glass Town and Angria sagas, the movement from prose to poetry signifies a change from the cynicism of prose with the public language of men to a much-softened language of a feminine poetic spirit, out of touch and out of time with the leadership demands made on Zamorna. This is not a portrait of a man travelling with guards or counsellors; rather, it is a very personal moment, a transitional image of a man stepping away from public demands to private yearning. Throughout the Glass Town tales, his earlier, Romantic poet self is evoked at significant moments to give voice to his interior world. Charlotte's use of the poetic form at such moments is a movement away from the linearity of prose narratives to a more holistic understanding of the self in a moment of quiet reflection on Beauty observed, admired and desired. The fragment invokes internalised awareness of a public life lived at odds with Zamorna's private desires.

Zamorna, both involved character and engaged narrator here, admits in his imagined confession to Mary, that "I […] watched thee gliding by" (3) but must keep himself from relieving her pain by going to her in her sorrow. Although she is surrounded by a "festal throng" (5) of people engaged in "joy & gladsome mirth" (8), Mary stands apart, like Zamorna who "stood apart" (2) to watch her. Mary has lost connection with the public world, retreating from those people around her, just as Zamorna aches for the private life he could have had. The stolen moment allows reflective time for the once Romantic poet to construct her as the Romantic ideal he believes her to be.

Cast as a fairy queen, her "unconscious majesty" (4) gives him pause in his silent observation; he sees her as "Titania left by her loved elfin King" (25). Shakespearean in allusion, Zamorna is Oberon to Mary's Titania, and Oberon's regret over the spell he has cast over Titania parallels Zamorna's torn feelings over Mary's banishment. Titania also refers to Ovid's *Metamorphoses* where he names the second generation of divine beings the Titans, thus inferring divinity upon her father, Northangerland. That said, both pairs of lovers – Shakespearean, Ovidian and/or Brontëan – are strongly tied to nature. He feels the wind moved and sees by "day-light airs through foliage play" (16) and her body "clothed in […] tunic green" (17), an image of potential fertility and playfulness. Her hair, wrapped with a "coronal of flowers around amid thy brow curls" (18) and with a "lily-wand" (19), places Mary as a fée of power, but ephemeral in nature – she may disappear once the magic moment has passed, or cast herself into darkness from despair given their separation. For now, Zamorna sees her as an otherworldly Beauty. He encourages her to "shake off the lily-wreaths that hide those braids of golden hair" to let her glory shine without fear of reprisal or immodesty. [10] While the "stars rose & glimmered one by

10   See 1 Corinthians 13-15 (KJV): "Judge in yourselves: is it comely that a woman pray unto God uncovered? Doth not even nature itself teach you, that, if a man have long hair, it is a shame unto him? But if a woman have long hair, it is a glory to her: for *her* hair is given her for a covering."

one/Of many a sweet wild tale of faerie" (22-23). In a garden's "placid bower" (29) she is

> *Curtained with tendrils of the eglantine*
> *~~Rose bud~~ Orchis & vetch, & spicy musk-rose creeping*
> *To join their blossoms with the sweet woodbine*
> *And for the fairy queen a veil to twine*
> *Moonlight* (31-35)

as she is "Called forth by dreams that of her lost love be" (38). The heavily-scented air, embroidered with the mixing fragrances of sweet briar and musk roses along with honeysuckle may be read in parallel poetic scenes where Oberon describes:

> *a bank where the wild thyme blows*
> *Where oxlips and the nodding violet grows,*
> *Quite over-canopied with luscious woodbine,*
> *With sweet musk-roses and with eglantine:*
> *There sleeps Titania sometime of the night.*

In addition to the Shakespearean correspondence, Charlotte's desiring Zamorna sees Mary's powerful feminine beauty as serene, sensuous, and colourful, all in contrast to the deplorably aggressive and devastating action he has taken to cast her out, an exile from love but radiant in her duty. At the same time as he sees her in what is akin to a Romantic dream vision, in reality, Mary and Zamorna are lovers kept apart by revenge politics, not by lack of love. To win against another man, Zamorna has had to abnegate a chivalric role: he has played the hand of a woman to win his game with a man.

There is, perhaps, an element of fear as he gazes at Mary, fear that he will succumb in his weakness to her strength. The sensuous nature that surrounds her leads Zamorna to describe Mary in language of brilliance, lightness, spirituality, grace and resolve – she is "calm" (4) with a "step that [. . .] fell like snow-flake to the earth" (6) – in juxtaposition with the decadent luxury of the "Robes, gems &

masques & tossing plumes" (7) in the background. Zamorna is keenly aware that she wears a "long lucid chain of orient pearls" (20) that signify both her love and her sadness. The image is multi-layered; most likely a gift from Zamorna, because in the early nineteenth century "pearls embellished more intimate or 'sentimental' jewellery to convey personal messages celebrating love or expressing grief", and there is also a connection to Southey. Zamorna equates Mary's pearls with the "tears alas from her closed eye-lids streaming" (37) down her gown, while in his "Elegy II" when Southey's poet approaches Delia, he describes tears that become pearls of grief:

> *She weeps, she weeps! Her eye with anguish swells,*
> *Some tale of sorry melts my feeling girl!*
> *NYMPHS! Catch the tears, and in your lucid shells*
> *Enclose them, EMBRYOS OF THE ORIENT PEARL.* (17-20)

Other reminders of devotion surround Mary throughout the fragment, including the "emerald ring" (55) she wears. Emeralds have historically been seen as symbols of love, compassion, harmony and abundance;[11] in addition, as a glimpse of possibility among the decaying ruins, there are "cushant doves" (44), or mourning doves, who mate for life and live quietly amongst the ivy. While Zamorna directs his gaze at physical embodiments of the strength of the bond between himself and Mary, he possibly senses the deep mourning grief that they each feel. He watches from afar because he is driven to build a nation that will, eventually, crumble.

There is an impending sense of loss as the poem's images move through the Lake District, where the "awful glooms among Helvellyns giant mass" (46) throws on "his subject [...] a mournful shadow" (41). Zamorna, as narrator, tells us that there are "many piles decay" (43) that are "ivy-veiled & grey/Old abbeys, antique monasteries, proud halls & stately towers/All buried" (44-46) and "all sadly mouldering" (48). After passing through cycles of life

11   Indeed, *Prince Albert proposed to Queen Victoria with an emerald ring.*

including "Through winter's night, through summers day, dim autumn & sweet spring" (47) These man-made monuments, odes to male-centred philosophies of religion, war and politics, have now become broken and decayed – through the "howling blast" (48) of patriarchal history – into a kind of sterility that stands in contrast to the fecund nature and promise that surrounds the feminine portrait of Mary.

The fragment then leaps in time to where a "hundred years have sped" leaving unclear the realistic footing of the fairy vision near the holy "white Island of the west" (50). Perhaps time dramatically shifts because once Zamorna sees Mary, he confesses "upon me stole came fell/A dream that bore my spirit far away" (13-14) to the "Grand Indian forest shade" (53) where the air is filled with intoxicating "spicy breezes" (54) while "there the festal dance was graced with thy loved ??? king/By the Deep Ganges" under the "Indian moon's refulgent beam" (56-58). His thoughts take the couple out of the particularity of their impossible circumstances where the public conflicts with the private.

Once away from Glass Town, the exoticism of the surroundings – although not unknown in the Glass Town tales – are here entwined with Zamorna's lasting passion for Mary. Their potentially healing reunion might be found in a sensual reawakening of his long-buried artistic, loving spirit, one that is embodied in his choice of this poetic utterance to express his spiritual needs. In his longing, he sees her infinite, steadfast and pure "love that glows in those fair eyes as their dark lashes fall" (61) knowing that when "Sweetest look up & smile on me, I claim thee for mine own" (63).

Their deep emotional attachment evokes the Romantic supernatural when Mary seems, to the narrator Zamorna, to understand through inexplicable capacity, that "little think'st that I am nigh, thou'rt seeking for me now/I know it by that gentle sigh & by that anxious brow" (67-68) but he reassures her in his internalised conversation that she is, indeed, "Titania brightest fairest, best star of my kingdom's sky" (70).[12] Zamorna despairs at how "woe can touch the fairy-queen" (52) and knows that mutual comfort might yet be found. He wishes he could comfort her, that she could "Turn to the Haven of thy rest, for I am standing by/&now wherever thou mayst roam by hill by stream by tree/My bosom is thy happy home, my arms thy refuge be" (70-72). The appearance of their wretched plight – one of lovers torn apart by circumstances outside their control – is far from the truth of Zamorna's self-imposed, destructive revenge. Zamorna may, if he so chooses, end both their suffering if he would only sacrifice his need for vengeance. These acts of renunciation and reunion are, perhaps, only possible in the realm of his dreams.

This new poetic episode – a fragment of glass – demonstrates that Mary, his other-worldly fairy queen, is the only woman who entirely captures Zamorna's heart and imagination. Although he might be scandalous for his numerous mistresses, and his two previous wives, he always returns to Mary because – no matter his faults – she still sees him in the light of his early Romantic persona,[13] not in his Byronic turn as a craven leader, just as Zamorna still sees her as his only poetic muse: Beauty personified. It could be argued that Mary follows him because he is the Romantic, solitary man who is alienated even when amongst his subjects. Like a looking glass, in her strength, Mary reflects Zamorna back to himself as the "poet who surpassed Byron, the warrior who equaled my father, the hero who counted life as lighter than dust when weighed in the balance with glory".

Charlotte gives us here a moment that is important for at least two reasons. Firstly, the author is not trying to suppress her admiration for the charismatic hero but indulging it. Secondly, she allows for the possibility that Zamorna wishes to return to an earlier

---

12 This image of woman as both possessed and desiring is reminiscent of the complex potential of a woman's love to embrace negative male nature in Samuel Taylor Coleridge's "woman wailing for her demon lover" (16). is from "Kubla Khan; Or, A Vision in a Dream. A Fragment" published in *Christabel, Kubla Khan, and the Pains of Sleep* (1816).

13 The episode most striking is in the novella, *Caroline Vernon*, for its retreat to the idealised pastoral or "country plainness" (Brontës 234) is when they both retreat to a farmstead, a kind of reversal of "Michael" (1800) by Wordsworth. Rather than seek out riches in the city like Michael's heir, Zamorna wishes to retreat from the perils of the city to the simplicity of Nature.

state of desire and to his Beauty – he longs for Mary in a poetic revelation of his capability for enduring love and in regret for the young poet his life left behind.

Once in Charlotte Brontë's early juvenile writing, Lord Charles Wellesley muses, "It seemed as if I was a non-existent shadow, that I neither spoke, eat [sic], imagined or lived of myself, but I was the mere idea of some other creature's brain". This moment of reflection shatters the distance between character and author since Charlotte is behind the pseudonym, hoping to go through the looking glass to the worlds open to literary men. How fortunate I have been to be involved in this historic moment; to read Charlotte Brontë's recovered juvenile writing, if only fragments of glass, reminds us that to recover pieces is a chance to construct a window to the past.

References

Alexander, Christine. "Early Ambitions: Charlotte Brontë, Henry Kirke White and Robert Southey." *Brontë Studies*. 43.1(2018): pp. 14-31.

Alexander, Christine. "Introduction" in Brontës. *Tales of Glass Town, Angria, and Gondal: Selected Writings*. Ed. Christine Alexander. Oxford: Oxford University Press, 2010. pp. xiii-xliii.

Alexander, Christine and McMaster, Juliet. Eds. *The Child Writer from Austen to Woolf*. Cambridge: Cambridge University Press, 2005.

Alexander, Christine. "Defining and representing literary juvenilia" in *The Child Writer from Austen to Woolf*. Eds. Christine Alexander and Juliet McMaster. Cambridge: Cambridge University Press, 2005. pp. 70-97.

Alexander, Christine. *The Early Writings of Charlotte Brontë*. Oxford: Blackwell, 1983.

Alexander, Christine. "Angria Revalued: Charlotte Brontë's Efforts to Free Herself from her Juvenilia." 1980. *The Brontë Sisters Critical Assessments Volume I*. Ed. Eleanor McNees. 1996. pp. 442-450.

Barker, Juliet. *The Brontës: Wild Genius on the Moors: The Story of a Literary Family*. London: Pegasus Books, 2012.

Brontës. *Tales of Glass Town, Angria, and Gondal: Selected Writings*. Ed. Christine Alexander. Oxford: Oxford University Press, 2010.

Brontë, Charlotte. *Jane Eyre*. 1847. Oxford: Oxford, 2008.

Brontë, Charlotte. *The Letters of Charlotte Brontë Volume One 1829-1847*. Ed. Margaret Smith. Oxford: Oxford University Press, 1995.

Brontë, Charlotte. *An Edition of the Early Writings of Charlotte Brontë Volume III 1834-1835*. Ed. Christine Alexander. Oxford: Basil Blackwell, 1991.

Brontë, Charlotte. *An Edition of the Early Writings of Charlotte Brontë Volume II 1833-1834*. Ed. Christine Alexander. Oxford: Basil Blackwell, 1991.

Brontë, Charlotte. *An Edition of the Early Writings of Charlotte Brontë Volume I 1826-1832*. Ed. Christine Alexander. Oxford: Basil Blackwell, 1987.

Brontë, Charlotte. "The Return of Zamorna." in *The Miscellaneous and Unpublished Writings of Charlotte and Patrick Branwell Brontë in Two Volumes. Volume II*. Eds. Thomas Wise, John Symington and Charles Hatfield. Oxford: Shakespeare Head Press, 1938. pp. 281-314.

Brontë, Charlotte. "Zamorna's Exile." 1836. in *Legends of Angri*a. Ed. Fannie Ratchford. New Haven: Yale University Press, 1933. pp. 111-147.

Coleridge, Samuel Taylor. "Kubla Khan; Or, A Vision in a Dream. A Fragment." In *Christabel, Kubla Khan, and the Pains of Sleep*. London: John Murray, 1816. pp. 49-58.

Gaskell, Elizabeth. *The Letters of Mrs. Gaskell*. Eds. J. A. V. Chapple and Arthur Pollard. Oxford: Oxford University Press, 1997.

Gaskell, Elizabeth. *The Life of Charlotte Brontë*. 1857. Ed. Alan Shelston. London: Penguin, 1975.

Glen, Heather. "Experiments in Fiction: Charlotte Brontë's Last Angrian Tales." *Women's Writing*. 14.1 (May 2007): pp. 4-22.

Glen, Heather. "Background to Angria." In Brontë, Charlotte. *Tales of Angria*. Ed. Heather Glen. London: Penguin, 2006. pp. lviii-lx.

Green, Dudley. *Patrick Brontë: Father of Genius*. Stroud: Nonsuch Publishing, 2008.

Langbauer, Laurie. *The Juvenile Tradition*. Oxford: Oxford University Press, 2016.

Keats, John. "The Eve of St. Agnes." In *Lamia, Isabella, The Eve of St. Agnes and other poems*. London: Taylor and Hessey, 1820. pp. 81-107.

Langbauer, Laurie. "Prolepsis and the Tradition of Juvenile Writing: Henry Kirke White and Robert Southey." *PMLA*. 128.4(2013): pp. 888-906.

Maier, Sarah E. "Charlotte Bronte (1816–1855): (Un)Masked Author to Mythic Woman" in *Biographical Misrepresentations of British Women Writers: A Hall of Mirrors and the Long Nineteenth Century*. Ed. Brenda Ayres. London: Palgrave, 2017. pp. 211-229.

McMaster, Juliet. "What Daisy knew: the epistemology of the child writer" in *The Child Writer from Austen to Woolf*. Eds. Christine Alexander and Juliet McMaster. Cambridge: Cambridge University Press, 2005. pp. 51-69.

Ratchford, Fannie. "Introduction to 'Zamorna's Exile'." *Legends of Angria*. New Haven: Yale University Press, 1933. pp. 103-109.

Ratchford, Fannie. "The Brontës' Web of Dreams." 1931. *The Brontë Sisters Critical Assessments Volume I*. Ed. Eleanor McNees, 1996. pp. 423-436.

Sanders, Valerie and Emma Butcher. "'Mortal Hostility': Masculinity and fatherly conflict in the Glass Town and Angrian sagas" in *Charlotte Brontë from the Beginnings: New Essays from the Juvenilia to the Major Works*. Eds. Judith E. Pike and Lucy Morrison. New York: Routledge, 2017. pp. 59-72.

Shakespeare, William. "A Midsummer-Night's Dream" in *The Complete Works of William Shakespeare*. London: Abbey Library, 1977. pp. 175-195.

Southey, Robert. *The Complete Poetical Works of Robert Southey, LL.D. (later poet laureate)*. New York: Appleton, 1846.

Victoria and Albert Museum. *Pearls*. Exhibition Introduction. London. 21 September 2013 – 19 January 2014. vam.ac.uk/content/exhibitions/exhibition-pearls/about-the-exhibition/

White, Henry Kirk. *The Remains of Henry Kirke White. Of Nottingham, Late of St. John's College, Cambridge; with an Account of his Life in Two Volumes. Volume One. Fourth Edition. Ed. Robert Southey*. London: Longman, 1810.

Wesley, Rev. John. *Wesleyan Methodist Magazine Volume VIII*. London: J. Mason, 1829.

Williams, Meg Harris. "Book Magic: Aesthetic Conflicts in Charlotte Brontë's Juvenilia." *Nineteenth-Century Fiction*. 42.1 (June 1987). pp. 29-45.

REINVENTING HEAVEN

Ann-Marie Richardson

The impact of the Brontë's copy of
The Remains of Henry Kirke White upon
the ghosts of *Wuthering Heights*

The function of relics in recovering a lost past means Henry Kirke White's *Remains* presents a unique link to the daily life of the Brontës. However this study will demonstrate that the Brontës themselves also utilised this anthology to compensate for an absence: namely, that of their mother, Maria (1783-1821). This edition provides not only an insight into Maria's intelligence, but also a bridge between her motherless children and her memory.

This method of posthumous perception is strikingly similar to the most Gothic scene in Emily Brontë's *Wuthering Heights*: the (inadvertent) summoning of Catherine Earnshaw's ghost. Invoked by the disturbance of her library, this analysis will demonstrate how the Heights' phantom can be read as an extended metaphor for the role *Remains* played in invoking the "spirit" of Maria. Furthermore, this essay will conduct an in-depth comparison of *Remains* and Catherine's fictional relics, and how Kirke White's verse, specifically his seminal *Clifton Grove*, helped shape the primary plot of Emily's only novel.

Ann-Marie Richardson is a PhD candidate at the University of Liverpool. Her thesis, titled *Weaponised Imagination*, concentrates on sibling rivalry in nineteenth-century literary families, specifically the Rossettis and Brontës. Her current critical interest in Maria Brontë was generated when researching the role creative parents play in these early writings, which led to her ongoing study of the Brontë's edition of Henry Kirke White's *Remains* and *Poetical Works*.

Beside the fireside, a story is told of two lovers, prevented from being together by poverty and familial expectation. The pair defy the fates that wish to separate them, and yet, in our hero's three-year absence from home, the heroine marries the most eligible man in the county. Returning a self-made man and witnessing this betrayal, the hero torments the woman until she dies in delirium, not before having given birth to a child at exactly midnight. The tale concludes with the lovers haunting their childhood home for the rest of eternity.

While Brontë scholars and avid readers alike may identify this story as a rudimentary synopsis of Emily Brontë's *Wuthering Heights*, it is in fact an abridgment of Henry Kirke White's romance *Clifton Grove*.[1]

However, like Brontë's only novel, Kirke White's 'sketch in verse' is a far more nuanced portrayal of the importance of place; memory and romantic images contained within a gothic setting. Parallels in these motifs between the two works are equally uncanny, although *Wuthering Heights* extends and supplements this story to give the female protagonist, Cathy, a clearer defence than Kirke White's Margaret. Similarly, Heathcliff's dissolution is more layered than Kirke White's Bateman, although both are stoic, enigmatic and undesirable to all but their loves.

Patrick Brontë's pride in having attended St. John's College with the poet means that we know the Brontë siblings had knowledge of his work. However, with the retrieval of the Brontë's edition, we can now ascertain how exceedingly familiar the literary family was with his verse in their childhood, and the considerable impression his *Clifton Grove* had upon the nascent authoress, Emily Brontë. The hypothesis of this analysis is to outline in detail the profound similarities between these works, but also the effect the edition itself, as a tangible remnant of both Kirke White and Brontë's mother, had upon the structure and psyche of her seminal ghost story.

It is rare that we measure someone's life by their absence in the

Emily Brontë by Patrick Branwell Brontë, oil on canvas, c. 1833.

Branwell's portrait of Emily. Kirke White's poem, *Clifton Grove*, had a significant influence on her writing.

lives of others, but this is the legacy of the Brontë matriarch, Maria (1783-1821). Daphne du Maurier, in her partiality for the home county she and Maria shared, believed Emily to have been bequeathed her mother's "Cornish individuality and pride", despite never having seen the region (*Vanishing Cornwall*, 162). It is this self-assurance, du Maurier maintains, that would give Emily the courage to write a "coarse" novel like *Wuthering Heights*. The majority of biographers, however, believe it was Maria's premature death that was her most significant literary influence. Disregarding the support of Patrick and Aunt Branwell, Elizabeth Gaskell asserts that because "the little Brontës had been brought up motherless", they were "ignorant of the very nature of infancy" in its gaiety (*The Life of Charlotte Brontë*, 183). Her claims of neglect are emphasised so heavily, it is implied that Gaskell believes the motherless status of the Brontë sisters to have been necessary in order to forge the "uncouth" themes critics frequently accused them of. In a defence of their lack of femininity, Gaskell chalks it up to being deprived of a biological mother's influence. A writer first and a biographer second, Gaskell's account does often feel hyperbolic, as Samantha Ellis argues Gaskell "never let facts get in the way of a good story" (*Take Courage*, 88). However the eloquence of the portrayal of grief in the Brontë novels does exhibit some truth in her psychological reading. If we accept that the siblings' belief in a literary séance as an illusion of the desire that those they have lost remain a part of their home through the relics they have left behind, a closer reading reveals the influence of such vestiges.

Heathcliff's deep-rooted grief twenty years after Cathy's death results in some of the most eloquent passages in his speech, increased when he learns her ghost has returned to the Heights and tormented the stranger, Lockwood. In one of the most recognisable scenes of *Wuthering Heights*, Cathy's spectre smashes through the glass of her bedroom window, begging entry into her childhood home. Desperate to see her, Heathcliff attempts to copy Lockwood's actions on the night of the apparition and sleeps in her bed. He even rests his head on the pillow so he and the ghost might share, as they did as children when they hid from the interfering adults in her bedroom, saying: "I opened and closed (my eyes) a hundred times a night – to be always disappointed!" (242) His attempts to summon a spirit are fruitless and Heathcliff grows mad with desperation, even entreating: "hear me *this* time", implying that her spectre has ignored him on multiple occasions (23). Consequently, he resorts to profane methods to see Catherine again, desecrating her grave: "I saw her face again," he tells housekeeper Nelly, "it is hers yet" (240).

His idealised preservation of her in his memory is so complete, it is projected on to her body. Brontë scholar, Deborah Lutz, explores the progression of Heathcliff's scheme to disturb her grave, arguing the idea came from his time in her bedroom. Although the room is described as minimally furnished, the space is dominated by a box bed resembling "a larger oak case" (15) or, as Lutz suggests, a coffin, as he once again "gets into the dead Catherine's box" (*The Brontë Cabinet*, p.xx). This is where the ghost visited Lockwood that stormy night he needed a place to take refuge, yet despite Heathcliff's earlier entreaty that Catherine "(b)e with him always, take any form" (140), her new shape eludes him and he feels forced to invade her earthly territory increasingly, hoping to incite a vengeful poltergeist.

Although *Wuthering Heights* has long been marketed as a tale of love conquering death, despite vengeance often being the greatest provocation for the supernatural occurrences of the novel[2], it is the outsider, Lockwood, who Cathy haunts. This calls into question what act Lockwood commits to warrant the appearance of a phantom – and which aspect of his night in the box bed that Heathcliff overlooked. The answer is straightforward: unlike Heathcliff, who disturbs her very corpse, Lockwood disturbs her library.

Catherine's childhood box bed does not resemble a coffin so much as a small office or "select library", the design allowing for a small closet and a windowsill, which serves as a makeshift desk (15).

A box bed, as described by Emily in *Wuthering Heights*.

Photo courtesy Julie Akhurst, Ponden Hall

Famously carved into the windowsill are variations on Catherine's name, her juvenile graffiti alternating between the surnames of Earnshaw, Heathcliff and Linton. Upon the defaced shelf is a small collection of exercise books and testaments from Cathy's childhood, which Lockwood observes to be "mildewed" by age and in a "state of dilapidation" from heavy use. Within this small archive, almost every page of these volumes is filled with childish annotations, as Lockwood notes: "scarcely one chapter had escaped a pen-and-ink commentary" (15). Fascinated by the narrative of the conflicted childhood each individual scrawl weaves, Lockwood spends the night making sense of the juvenile writing until "a glare of white letters started from the dark" before Lockwood "as vivid as spectres – the air swarmed with Catherines" (15). Soon afterwards, a real spectre appears outside the window, on the other side of the shelved library, demanding access to the Heights. Where Heathcliff's words could not tempt the ghost, the written word has the power to summon her. Moreover, by reading the very words Cathy wrote as a child, Lockwood not only allows a clear picture to the personality of this previously unknown girl to emerge, but literally breathes life into the ghost.

Consider Lockwood's terrified struggle with the spectre: after her ghostly arm penetrates the glass of the bedroom window, Lockwood "pulled its wrist on to the broken pane, and rubbed it to and fro till the blood ran down and soaked the bedclothes" (20). This graphic image implies Cathy's ghost is tangible, capable of bleeding, contrary to popular Gothic assertion that spirits are incorporeal. For a brief moment, it seems the written word has not only triggered a visitation from a ghost, but returned Cathy to an earthly presence where she can draw blood and penetrate the window. Whether we read this as a nightmare or a poltergeist, this Gothic apex in the narrative alludes to the power of the written word in retrieving the author, in spite of evident boundaries. This emphasises the power the young Brontës attributed to the faded heirlooms bequeathed on the demise of a loved one.

Although this analysis will focus predominantly upon the death of the mother, the childhood loss of the elder Brontë sister, Maria, also shaped the elegiac passages of the siblings' literature and contributes to our reading of the Brontës' copy of the *Remains*. Maria, like the mother she was named after, would also leave a rare literary remnant of her existence in the Parsonage, as Charlotte's *History of the Year* (1829) observes. In this journal-like style, a twelve-year-old Charlotte Brontë details the advent of Brontë juvenilia as the siblings play with a box of soldiers belonging to Branwell. These toy legionnaires would famously lead to the creation of the Brontë siblings' first fictional characters. Prior to this, however, Charlotte explains that, at the time of writing, lying before her was an old geography book, which her father once loaned to her eldest sister. Four years after her sister's death, Charlotte peruses the book and observes:

> she (Maria) wrote on its blank leaf 'Papa lent me this book'. This book is a hundred and twenty years old.[3]

Her alternative diary continues to describe the busy goings-on of the Brontë house:

Anne, my younger sister (Maria was my eldest), is kneeling on a chair […] Emily is in the parlour, brushing the carpet. Papa and Branwell are gone to Keighley. Aunt is upstairs.

Maria's name is incorporated within the daily activities of the Parsonage so her memory could renew her presence there. This antique book is made a treasure not by its age, but by Maria's minor vandalism, a rare remnant of the sister whose writing would never be incorporated within the siblings' juvenilia.

Understandably, the sadness of this loss was increased for Charlotte as, by 1829, she had come to regard her surviving siblings as co-authors, the fellow Genii of the Glass Town Confederacy in their juvenilia. This activity was one her sisters, Maria and Elizabeth, would never be able to play a part in. Her written word, therefore, allows Charlotte to integrate her sister into both the Parsonage's daily activities and their play-writing, because she is no longer invisible. This resistance of invisibility through writing is one embodied in the ghost of *Wuthering Heights*, a literal presence formed from her absence.

It is intriguing therefore that Heathcliff, when describing his perpetual mourning for Cathy, acknowledges: "What is not connected with her to me? […] and what does not recall her? […] (t)he entire world is a dreadful collection of memoranda that she did exist, and that I have lost her!" (270).

By describing the nature of his grief in an almost materialistic fashion, we are reminded of the very few articles belonging to Maria that were left as mementoes for the Brontë children, due to the unforeseen but tragic consequence of the shipwreck which resulted in the loss of her belongings. Debatably, therefore, the most unfortunate aspect of *The Remains of Henry Kirke White* is the apparent lack of annotation by their mother herself. Although they knew the book to be hers, there were no echoes of her which her children could have read. While Maria cannot make her role

Once upon a time there was a king
whose name was ~~Ethelbert~~ Eleance
Who Governed all Caledonia his
disposition was was, warlike and
~~some~~ what tinged wi

The History of the ~~year~~

Once papa lent my Sister Maria
A Book it was an old Geography
and she wrote on it's Blank leaf
papa lent me this Book. the
Book is an hundred and twenty
years old it is at this moment
lying Before me while I write
this I am in the kitchin of
the parsonage house Haworth
July the servant is washing up
after Breakfast and Anne my
youngest Sister (Maria was my
eldest) is kneeling on a chair
looking at some cakes which Tabby
has been Baking for us. Emily
is in the parlour brushing it
~~papa~~ papa and Branwell are gone
March 12 1829

Charlotte's *History of the Year*, written in 1829 when she was thirteen.

in this book's history visible, Patrick uses his own writing to breathe life into her memory. Upon the flyleaf of the Brontë's edition, Patrick declares the book to have belonged to his "dearest wife" with the promise that it will "always be preserved". This need to maintain a sense of ownership after death, to sustain a literary presence, is echoed in Cathy's testament in *Wuthering Heights* as the flyleaf of her testament contains the declaration: "Catherine Earnshaw, her book" (15).

Watercolour portrait of Maria Brontë, née Branwell, as a young woman. The artist is unknown – it was later copied by Charlotte.

Patrick grants himself the custodianship of Maria's Kirke White memoir as his eldest daughter once did his geography book. Evidently Patrick, like his daughters, believed writing to be an opportunity for interaction with those they had loved and lost. Undoubtedly, this belief was strengthened when reading the *Remains*, which gave him the opportunity to peruse his friend's words as well as recall his wife's memory. His friendship with Kirke White is also upheld through his annotations. The poem *Solitude*, for instance, is one of the most heavily annotated pieces in the Brontë's edition, with Patrick's familiar handwriting from the flyleaf declaring the verse "Kirke White's chef d'oeuvre": his masterpiece.

The *Remains* was a two-fold memoriam for his wife and his fellow university sizar; his honour for having been acquainted with this poet is encapsulated in yet another annotation in which Patrick states he has "every reason to think that the praise bestowed upon him (White) […] was well merited". Reading, for Patrick, created a literary synthesis, both with Kirke White, the author, and Maria, the book's original owner.

Emily Brontë amplifies this practice by embodying memories as literal ghosts. The significance her father, and her sister Maria, placed upon ownership and identity is mirrored in Catherine's "select" library when she claims an exercise book as her own, as well as in her rehearsal of potential surnames. Being torn between Heathcliff and Edgar is embodied in her alternating between the surnames "Heathcliff" and "Linton", although such uncertainty is not reflected in her mother's book; we have already seen the importance of establishing identity that the Kirke White edition exemplifies. Surnames are even corrected in the correspondence section of the memoir. In a transcript of an 1805 letter to his mother, Kirke White explains that he has borrowed the bills from an economical fellow undergraduate in order to improve his spending. In Southey's careful edit, however, the "genteel" scholar's name is redacted to "Mr ***". Patrick, however, amends this, placing a small obelus (†) beside the omission and in the right-hand margin simply adds the note, "Brontë". Visibly proud of his association with Kirke

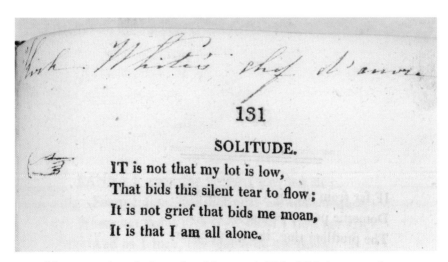

131

SOLITUDE.

IT is not that my lot is low,
That bids this silent tear to flow;
It is not grief that bids me moan,
It is that I am all alone.

One of the annotations declares that this poem is Kirke White's masterpiece.

White, Patrick wished to make it clear to his family that the respect was mutual, linking himself to the poet as well as his wife, both memories he wished to preserve.

However, although Lockwood was perusing Catherine's memories, he bore no memory of her himself. The within-and-without nature of Lockwood and Cathy's association – her personality only accessible to him through her memories and the recollections of others – parallels the emotional response Emily would have had to being able to communicate with her mother only through the literary remains she once owned, a tangible sense of Maria's intellect. Consequently, Emily, her siblings, and her father, would write upon the pages of the *Remains* in a posthumous collaboration with what remained of her mother. Their childish annotations responded to her favoured verses in order to form a one-sided intellectual conversation with her relics.

Equally, the siblings would allow instances from their daily life, as well as their early fiction, to spill over into marginalia of the *Remains*. Mathematical equations are penned down in the blank spaces, and miniscule, block letters, practising spelling in a childlike manner. The marginalia of the poem, *Solitude*, for instance, contains a deliberation of how to spell "piece/peice".

Psychologically, through this act, they are inviting the vestiges of their mother into their daily life, as Charlotte believed her *History of the Year* once did for her sister. Correspondingly, in Catherine's favourite books every gap is filled with her commentary, as Lockwood notes: "(s)ome were detached sentences; other parts took the form of a regular diary, scrawled in an unformed, childish hand" (15).

Ingenuous scribblings cover the pages of the *Remains* in a similar fashion. It is intriguing that Lockwood should uncover exercise books when the *Remains* doubled as a classroom jotter in such a manner, containing lessons in English, arithmetic and even shorthand. The shorthand was most likely to have been written by Patrick; Byrom shorthand being a common skill studied by

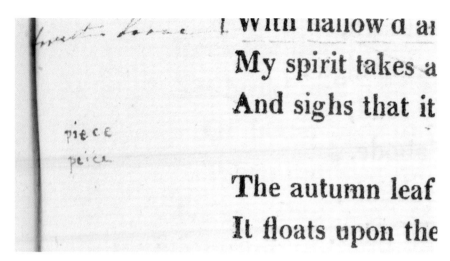

A debate over the spelling of 'piece' alongside the poem, *Solitude*.

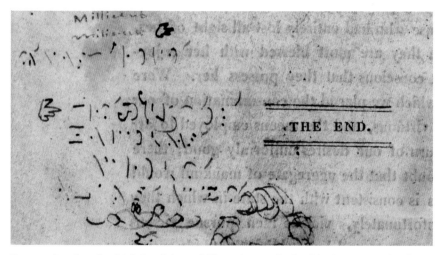

Byrom shorthand, which Patrick would have learnt during his time at Cambridge.

Oxbridge fellows. It is improbable that Emily and her sisters would have been able to interpret the passage, much as Lockwood struggles to decode the untidy hand of Cathy, which he describes as "faded hieroglyphics". The shorthand may have appeared as undecipherable as hieroglyphics for the untrained Emily, although Cathy's words were encrypted by the disordered penmanship of childhood rather than a specific mode of writing. Once Lockwood makes sense of

Cathy's hieroglyphics, he finds sporadic journal entries detailing a much more tempestuous daily life with her brother, describing him as "detestable" and "his conduct to Heathcliff is atrocious. – H. and I are going to rebel" (16).

Although more detailed than the occasional annotations of the Brontës, this insight into the daily routine is reminiscent of the Brontës' skill for effortlessly blending daily life and fiction, epitomised in Charlotte's *History of the Year* and Emily and Anne's Gondal diary papers. While these comparisons between the scribblings of Cathy and the Brontë children have, thus far, been subtle allusions, there is one piece of graffiti which draws the greatest admiration from Lockwood, and bears the strongest resemblance to the doodles of the *Remains*: "an excellent caricature of my friend Joseph", the Heights' sanctimonious servant, "…rudely yet powerfully sketched. An immediate interest kindled within me for the unknown Catherine" (17).

With pastimes in both writing and drawing, the Brontës' scribblings were guaranteed to include sketches, however the

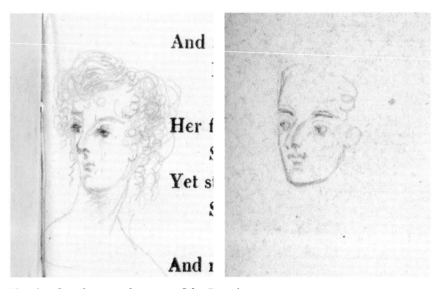

Sketches found among the pages of the *Remains*.

Note the similarity between the sketch (left) and the drawings in Branwell's Luddendenfoot notebook.

"rude yet powerful" drawings of the *Remains* are highly reminiscent of Charlotte and Branwell's early efforts. Moreover these rough sketches, drafted upon the memoir's pages, are highly reminiscent of Charlotte and Branwell's drafts of Angrian characters. Scribbled on the final page, for instance, is a sketch of a curly-haired young man with pointed features, highly similar to those coarse images doodled in Branwell Brontë's notebook during his work as a railway station master in Luddendenfoot. Illustrations of strong, determined young men, similar to this one, are the standard image of Charlotte and Branwell's Angrian anthology, frequently portraying the saga's most infamous heroes. Their juvenilia was a constant presence in the Brontë mindset, with doodles of characters absentmindedly etched in Branwell's Luddendenfoot notebook, as well as Charlotte's manuscript for the 1829 poem *Sunrise*.

The inclusion of Angrianesque images in the *Remains*, alongside the daily lessons, demonstrates an effort to merge Maria's relic with both fictional and non-fictional aspects of her children's lives. As Charlotte's *History of the Year* incorporated her sister's written word with the origins of their juvenilia, the drawings contained

Charlotte's manuscript for the 1829 poem *Sunrise*.

in the *Remains* encompasses both the book, and the memory of its owner, into the Glass Town corpus. The inclusion of their mother's memory in their early writing is highly significant as the Brontës initially considered their juvenilia as a private recreation amongst themselves. Their pocket-sized 'novels' and miniscule handwriting, many biographers maintain[4], demonstrate their efforts to keep adult eyes from reading their work, and yet, in their desire to know their lost mother better, the boundaries between imagination and a literary afterlife are blurred, as they are in *Wuthering Heights*.

Charlotte's *History of the Year* once again provides insight to their early mentality as she describes the plays both she and Emily are currently writing, based upon the adventures of these wooden soldiers, which the sisters christen "bed plays". "Bed plays", Charlotte explains "means secret plays they are very nice ones all our plays are very strange ones [sic.]". Like so many children, their bedrooms were regarded as their most private sanctuary, far from the cares of the everyday life and chores portrayed elsewhere in Charlotte's diary piece. Although far from secretive, the children's beds are highly private spaces where their imagination can be unreserved, as in dreams. We also learn in *History of the Year* that Emily and Charlotte "Jumped out of bed [sic.]" when Branwell enters with those seminal soldiers, thus the bedroom becomes the hub of their creativity.

Suddenly, the appearance of the ghost of *Wuthering Heights* through the window of the "box bed" is given new meaning: not only is the spirit bidden by the written word, but her literary summoning takes place in the foundations of the Brontë fiction: the bed. The design of the box bed exaggerates the security Emily and her siblings would have felt when building their imagined worlds in their bedroom. The fact that the oak case's cut-outs resemble coach windows implies the transporting power of the bed (15), and its binary role as a small library is further proof of the space's apocryphal function.

Emily constructs an all encompassing edifice where Lockwood can close the bed's panel and create a "room within a room", embodying the escapist power of imagination as Lockwood closes the panels and feels "secure against the vigilance of Heathcliff, and every one else" (15). Thus, the bed occupies a space between the harsh realities of a Heathcliff-dominated Heights and the window through which the ghost enters. An in-between – not entirely separate, yet not entirely included – between earth and heaven.

Deborah Lutz observes this purgatorial aspect of the box bed in Heathcliff's hopes that Cathy's ghost will visit him: "believing he can find her there […] (h)e perishes himself, and the novel hints that the bed provides a portal to another sphere, the one of ghosts" (*The Brontë Cabinet*, xx). Her spirit however, is not the ethereal, ungraspable, phantom we have been taught to expect, but a being formed of memories and writing.

The Brontë children believed fiction to be a conduit for the spirits of those they have lost and, with Patrick's encouragement, they studied those few articles their mother left behind, the majority of which were pieces of literature. Charlotte, in a letter to Hartley Coleridge, for instance, recalls a select number of issues of the *Lady's Magazine* being among her mementos retrieved from the sea.[5] Unfortunately, this compendium of publications did not survive her youth as, Charlotte sadly recollects: "(o)ne black day my father burnt them because they contained foolish love-stories". We have seen in his evident cherishing of the *Remains*, Patrick was determined to preserve his wife's memory. Thus, the fact he would rob himself – and his children – of a rare reminder of Maria shows the extent of his heartache.

Emily, in a somewhat bitter tone, mimics this incineration of romance in *Wuthering Heights*, as an embarrassed Catherine Jr. entreats Nelly to burn some love correspondence between herself and Linton Heathcliff, which she believes to be too romantic to be proper: "If I consent to burn them," Nelly asks, "will you promise faithfully neither to send nor receive a letter again?" (190). The immaturity of the second Catherine in this scene is heavily exaggerated, focusing on her "girlish" and "babyish" character, and the "entreaties that I (Nelly) would burn them – do anything rather than show them" (190). This sardonic comment of "do anything rather than show them" appears to be an echo of the acrimony Emily and her sisters must have towards their father when he destroyed the magazines. The significance Emily placed on her mother's lost possessions is seen here in Nelly's use, albeit cynically, of the descriptor "treasure" when referring to the missives. The term is also used in Lockwood's narrative as he describes the annotations in the first Cathy's exercise books as "quite the treasure" (17). What else would a young writer call those valuables retrieved from the sea but "treasures", those articles once belonging to her mother made precious by her death and their rarity? Why then would Patrick take these magazines, of extreme sentimental value, away from his children?

We can better comprehend his perception when we consider which of Maria's remnants the children were permitted to read. While they were actively encouraged to read Kirke White's verse as a testament to their mother's erudite nature, anything which broached upon their romantic connection caused Patrick to grow sensitive. In another recollection of Maria's literary legacy, Charlotte recalls perusing her mother's letters, written during her courtship with Patrick in 1812. Reading her

Patrick Brontë as a young man.

lengthy declarations of loyalty to Patrick, Charlotte describes having observed a sense of "refinement, a constancy, a modesty, a sense, a gentleness […] indescribable"[6] in her mother. However, she would not read this telling picture of her mother's personality until 1850 when Patrick hands her a "little packet of letters". Immediately, our sympathy goes out to Charlotte's deceased siblings, even more so when Charlotte specifies this is the "first time" she has been allowed to hold the letters. Charlotte must have understood the magnitude of it, with her siblings not being there to share the moment with her. Evidently, while Patrick wished his children to know Maria as a vibrant woman, he was extremely protective of their personal relationship. It was not until all but one of their children had died that he felt able to share their private romance.

Charlotte had to wait until all her siblings were dead before her father allowed her access to her mother's letters.

This caginess is echoed in the second Catherine's fear that her father, Edgar Linton, will discover the love letters: "Don't tell papa. You have not told papa, Ellen? Say you have not?" (189). Edgar's sensitivity to sentimentality is mirrored in his reticence to speak of Catherine Earnshaw to her daughter, mimicking Patrick's own reserve. Although the *Lady's Magazine*, like Kirke White's memoir, contained no examples of Maria's own writing, the very presence of love stories became too much for her widower. Through the ghost of Cathy, however, Emily vents her frustration of being kept from fully knowing her own parents' love story.

Without their mother to share the tale, the sole first-hand account of their family's story lay with their reluctant father. However Emily could call upon a past incarnation of Patrick, much as Lockwood does with the books of Cathy's youth, to understand their story better. Rare insights into her parents' strong passions were contained in yet more literature: her father's own poetry.

During their courtship, Patrick celebrated his relationship with Maria in his poem, *Lines, Addressed to a Lady, on her Birth-Day –* "'Maria,' – "let us walk, and breathe, the morning air" (l.51), – and in another poem, *Kirkstall Abbey*[7], marking the northern ruin where he proposed:

> The shapeless openings spread a solemn gloom,
> Recal the thoughtful mind, down to the silent tomb [sic.],
> And bid us for another world prepare.
> (ll.87-89).

Emily appears to respond to her father's romantic verse in her poetic pre-cursor to *Wuthering Heights*, a tale of the Gondalian Lord Alfred who, after dying on a distant battlefield, returns to haunt his homestead: *Aspin Castle*[8]. Emily's poem, *Written in Aspin Castle*, portrays the ghost of Lord Alfred haunting his family home, frequently sighted by the rustics who surround it:

> …his spirit unforgiven
> Wanders unsheltered shut from heaven
> An outcast for eternity
> (ll.81-83).

These lines read as an antecedent to Catherine's dream of ascending to heaven in *Wuthering Heights*: "heaven did not seem to be home; and I broke my heart with weeping to come back to earth; and the angels were so angry that they flung me out into the middle of the heath on the top of Wuthering Heights" (66).

Cathy favours her earthly home to that of heaven, because it is on earth she can be with Heathcliff. Equally, Patrick's romantic poetry contemplates the inevitable lapse of time which threatens to take his lover from him, admittedly not as soon as fate decided. His poem, *Verses, Sent to a Lady on her Birth-Day*[9] mourns that age and death will eventually mar her image:

Full soon, your eyes of sparkling blue
And velvet lips, of scarlet hue,
Discoloured, may decay
(ll.16-18)

However, Patrick concludes that someone so effervescent on earth can only be made more so in heaven, where:

. . . dressed in robes of heavenly light,
You'll raise angelic strains.
(ll.65-66)

The heavenly exile, Lord Alfred, appears to mimic the noblewoman for whom he was fighting when he was alive, known in Gondal fiction as A.G.A. It was in service of this woman that Lord Alfred wished to be remembered, yet she too has died:

Those eyes are dust – those lips are clay –
That form is mouldered all away
(ll.84-85)

Emily mirrors Patrick's language – but not his sentiments – as it is not in heaven that her characters are reunited but in this literary limbo she creates, represented by the inner-sanctum of the box bed. The ghost's face at the window not only represents the veil between this tangible world and the next, but the smashing of the glass – following the reading of Cathy's work – demonstrates how the act of literary interaction can cause the veil to fall. Recital of the written word is equally key in Emily's poem. By mimicking Patrick's language, she is demonstrating to him the only "visions" of her mother with which she has been acquainted: her death and her indirect literary presence. If she can only know her mother in a literary capacity, and even then not directly, Emily imagines for herself an alternate literary dimension in which she can communicate with her lost mother through the literature she loved.

CLIFTON GROVE.

A Sketch in Verse.

LO ! in the west, fast fades the lingering light,
And day's last vestige takes its silent flight.
No more is heard the woodman's measur'd stroke
Which, with the dawn, from yonder dingle broke;
No more, hoarse clamouring o'er the uplifted head,
The crows assembling, seek their wind-rock'd bed;
Still'd is the village hum—the woodland sounds
Have ceas'd to echo o'er the dewy grounds,
And general silence reigns, save when below,
The murmuring Trent is scarcely heard to flow;
And save when, swung by 'nighted rustic late,
Oft, on its hinge, rebounds the jarring gate:
Or, when the sheep bell, in the distant vale,
Breathes its wild music on the downy gale.

Now, when the rustic wears the social smile,
Releas'd from day and its attendant toil,
And draws his household round their evening fire,
And tells the oft-told tales that never tire:
Or, where the town's blue turrets dimly rise,
And manufacture taints the ambient skies,
The pale mechanic leaves the labouring loom,
The air-pent hold, the pestilential room,
And rushes out impatient to begin
The stated course of customary sin:

The opening verses of Henry Kirke White's *Clifton Grove.*

In her determination to form an image of her mother, she perused and interacted with *The Remains of Henry Kirke White*, and it is in his *Clifton Grove* that she finds a "kindred spirit", in every sense of the word. Having established the parallels in plot between this piece and *Wuthering Heights*, it is hardly likely Kirke White's *Clifton Grove* would be spared from the childish scrawls of the Brontë marginalia.

The pages are predominantly unaltered, aside from the saturation marks left behind from the memoir's time at sea. However there are two miniscule doodles which help us to understand the impact of the poem upon the Brontës' formative years. The first diminutive scribble is difficult to see clearly, but upon closer examination the sketch appears to depict a small gate, imagined as two small posts held together by a cross. The second is much more obscure, the messy hand appears to have roughly etched a rectangular shape – laying vertically in line with Kirke White's stanzas – with some small, unusual shapes pushing up vertically from its base, like the sails of a Viking ship. Although the doodles are much more challenging to interpret than the vast majority of the marginalia, it is their placement within Kirke White's writing which makes them so intriguing. Unlike the casual illustrations dotted across the pages in an unpractised manner, these sketches are strategically placed, marking the middle of one stanza and the end of another, respectively, in the space of seven pages.

The "gate" sketch, interrupts a verse in which we are told of the "far-famed Clifton Maid" (l.252) which inspired Kirke White's poem. Based upon folklore[10], the Fair Maid of Clifton, known in her own era by the name "Margaret" was considered the most beautiful woman of the county, if not all of England. Nottingham's answer to Helen of Troy, Kirke White depicts how Margaret was approached by many men who "confess'd in private his peculiar pain" (l.254), yet she "express'd disdain" (l.267) for all but her beloved, Bateman. It is at the commencement of these lines which the "gate" doodle marks:

> Yet not to all the maid express'd disdain;
> Her Bateman loved, nor loved the youth in vain.
> Full oft, low whispering o'er these arching boughs,
> The echoing vault responded to their vows,
> As here deep hidden from the glare of day,
> Enamour'd oft, they took their secret way.
> (267-272)

Far from these smiling fields, a rover went,
O'er distant lands, in search of ease to roam,
A self-will'd exile from his native home.

Yet not to all the maid express'd disdain,
Her BATEMAN lov'd, nor lov'd the youth in vain.
Full oft, low whispering o'er these arching boughs,
The echoing vault responded to their vows,
As here deep hidden from the glare of day,
Enamour'd oft, they took their secret way.

The 'gate' sketch.

And many an infant at its mother's breast,
Started dismayed, from its unthinking rest.
And even now, upon the heath forlorn,
They shew the path, down which the fair was borne,
By the fell demons, to the yawning wave,
Her own, and murder'd lover's, mutual grave.

Such is the tale, so sad, to memory dear,
Which oft in youth has charm'd my listening ear,
That tale, which bade me find redoubled sweets
In the drear silence of these dark retreats;

The Viking boat sketch.

CLIFTON GROVE

Henry Kirke White

Lo! in the west, fast fades the lingering light,
And day's last vestige takes its silent flight.
No more is heard the woodman's measured stroke,
Which with the dawn from yonder dingle broke;
No more, hoarse clamouring o'er the uplifted head,
The crows assembling seek their wind-rock'd bed;
Still'd is the village hum-the woodland sounds
Have ceased to echo o'er the dewy grounds,
And general silence reigns, save when below
The murmuring Trent is scarcely heard to flow;
And save when, swung by 'nighted rustic late,
Oft, on its hinge, rebounds the jarring gate;
Or when the sheep-bell, in the distant vale,
Breathes its wild music on the downy gale.

Now, when the rustic wears the social smile,
Released from day and its attendant toil,
And draws his household round their evening fire,
And tells the ofttold tales that never tire;
Or, where the town's blue turrets dimly rise,
And manufacture taints the ambient skies,
The pale mechanic leaves the labouring loom,
The air-pent hold, the pestilential room,
And rushes out, impatient to begin
The stated course of customary sin:
Now, now my solitary way I bend
Where solemn groves in awful state impend:
And cliffs, that boldly rise above the plain,
Bespeak, bless'd Clifton! thy sublime domain.
Here lonely wandering o'er the sylvan bower,
I come to pass the meditative hour;
To bid awhile the strife of passion cease,
And woo the calms of solitude and peace.
And oh! thou sacred Power, who rear'st on high
Thy leafy throne where wavy poplars sigh!
Genius of woodland shades! whose mild control
Steals with resistless witchery to the soul,
Come with thy wonted ardour, and inspire
My glowing bosom with thy hallow'd fire.
And thou, too, Fancy, from thy starry sphere,
Where to the hymning orbs thou lend'st thine ear,
Do thou descend, and bless my ravish'd sight,
Veil'd in soft visions of serene delight.
At thy command the gale that passes by
Bears in its whispers mystic harmony.
Thou wavest thy wand, and lo! what forms appear!
On the dark cloud what giant shapes career!
The ghosts of Ossian skim the misty vale,
And hosts of sylphids on the moonbeams sail.

This gloomy alcove darkling to the sight,
Where meeting trees create eternal night;
Save, when from yonder stream the sunny ray,
Reflected, gives a dubious gleam of day;
Recalls, endearing to my alter'd mind,
Times, when beneath the boxen hedge reclined,
I watch'd the lapwing to her clamorous brood;
Or lured the robin to its scatter'd food;
Or woke with song the woodland echo wild,
And at each gay response delighted smiled.
How oft, when childhood threw its golden ray
Of gay romance o'er every happy day,
Here, would I run, a visionary boy,
When the hoarse tempest shook the vaulted sky,
And, fancy-led, beheld the Almighty's form
Sternly careering on the eddying storm;
And heard, while awe congeal'd my inmost soul,
His voice terrific in the thunders roll.
With secret joy I view'd with vivid glare
The vollied lightnings cleave the sullen air;
And, as the warring winds around reviled,
With awful pleasure big,—I heard and smiled.
Beloved remembrance!—Memory which endears
This silent spot to my advancing years,
Here dwells eternal peace, eternal rest,
In shades like these to live is to be bless'd.
While happiness evades the busy crowd,
In rural coverts loves the maid to shroud.
And thou too, Inspiration, whose wild flame
Shoots with electric swiftness through the frame,
Thou here dost love to sit with upturn'd eye,
And listen to the stream that murmurs by,
The woods that wave, the gray owl's silken flight,
The mellow music of the listening night.
Congenial calms more welcome to my breast
Than maddening joy in dazzling lustre dress'd,
To Heaven my prayers, my daily prayers I raise,
That ye may bless my unambitious days,
Withdrawn, remote, from all the haunts of strife,
May trace with me the lowly vale of life,
And when her banner Death shall o'er me wave,
May keep your peaceful vigils on my grave.
Now as I rove, where wide the prospect grows,
A livelier light upon my vision flows.
No more above the embracing branches meet,
No more the river gurgles at my feet,
But seen deep down the cliff's impending side,
Through hanging woods, now gleams its silver tide.
Dim is my upland path,—across the green

Fantastic shadows fling, yet oft between
The chequer'd glooms the moon her chaste ray sheds,
Where knots of bluebells droop their graceful heads.
And beds of violets, blooming 'mid the trees,
Load with waste fragrance the nocturnal breeze.

Say, why does Man, while to his opening sight
Each shrub presents a source of chaste delight,
And Nature bids for him her treasures flow,
And gives to him alone his bliss to know,
Why does he pant for Vice's deadly charms?
Why clasp the syren Pleasure to his arms?
And suck deep draughts of her voluptuous breath,
Though fraught with ruin, infamy, and death?
Could he who thus to vile enjoyment clings
Know what calm joy from purer sources springs;
Could he but feel how sweet, how free from strife,
The harmless pleasures of a harmless life,
No more his soul would pant for joys impure,
The deadly chalice would no more allure,
But the sweet potion he was wont to sip
Would turn to poison on his conscious lip.

Fair Nature! thee, in all thy varied charms,
Fain would I clasp for ever in my arms!
Thine are the sweets which never, never sate,
Thine still remain through all the storms of fate.
Though not for me, 'twas Heaven's divine command
To roll in acres of paternal land,
Yet still my lot is bless'd, while I enjoy
Thine opening beauties with a lover's eye.

Happy is he, who, though the cup of bliss
Has ever shunn'd him when he thought to kiss,
Who, still in abject poverty or pain,
Can count with pleasure what small joys remain:
Though were his sight convey'd from zone to zone,
He would not find one spot of ground his own,
Yet as he looks around, he cries with glee,
These bounding prospects all were made for me:
For me yon waving fields their burden bear,
For me yon labourer guides the shining share,
While happy I in idle ease recline,
And mark the glorious visions as they shine.
This is the charm, by sages often told,
Converting all it touches into gold.
Content can soothe where'er by fortune placed,
Can rear a garden in the desert waste.

How lovely, from this hill's superior height,
Spreads the wide view before my straining sight!
O'er many a varied mile of lengthening ground,
E'en to the blue-ridged hill's remotest bound,

My ken is borne; while o'er my head serene
The silver moon illumes the misty scene:
Now shining clear, now darkening in the glade,
In all the soft varieties of shade.

Behind me, lo! the peaceful hamlet lies,
The drowsy god has seal'd the cotter's eyes.
No more, where late the social faggot blazed,
The vacant peal resounds, by little raised,
But locked in silence, o'er Arion's star
The slumbering Night rolls on her velvet car:
The church bell tolls, deep sounding down the glade,
The solemn hour for walking spectres made;
The simple ploughboy, wakening with the sound,
Listens aghast, and turns him startled round,
Then stops his ears, and strives to close his eyes,
Lest at the sound some grisly ghost should rise.
Now ceased the long, the monitory toll,
Returning silence stagnates in the soul;
Save when, disturbed by dreams, with wild affright,
The deep mouth'd mastiff bays the troubled night:
Or where the village alehouse crowns the vale,
The creaking signpost whistles to the gale.
A little onward let me bend my way,
Where the moss'd seat invites the traveller's stay.
That spot, oh! yet it is the very same;
That hawthorn gives it shade, and gave it name:
There yet the primrose opes its earliest bloom,
There yet the violet sheds its first perfume,
And in the branch that rears above the rest
The robin unmolested builds its nest.
'Twas here, when hope, presiding o'er my breast,
In vivid colours every prospect dress'd:
'Twas here, reclining, I indulged her dreams,
And lost the hour in visionary schemes.
Here, as I press once more the ancient seat,
Why, bland deceiver! not renew the cheat!
Say, can a few short years this change achieve,
That thy illusions can no more deceive!
Time's sombrous tints have every view o'erspread,
And thou too, gay seducer, art thou fled?

Though vain thy promise, and the suit severe,
Yet thou couldst guile Misfortune of her tear,
And oft thy smiles across life's gloomy way
Could throw a gleam of transitory day.
How gay, in youth, the flattering future seems;
How sweet is manhood in the infant's dreams;
The dire mistake too soon is brought to light.
And all is buried in redoubled night.
Yet some can rise superior to the pain,
And in their breasts the charmer Hope retain;
While others, dead to feeling, can survey,

Unmoved, their fairest prospects fade away:
But yet a few there be,—too soon o'ercast!
Who shrink unhappy from the adverse blast,
And woo the first bright gleam, which breaks the gloom,
To gild the silent slumbers of the tomb.
So in these shades the early primrose blows,
Too soon deceived by suns and melting snows:
So falls untimely on the desert waste,
Its blossoms withering in the northern blast.

Now pass'd whate'er the upland heights display,
Down the steep cliff I wind my devious way;
Oft rousing, as the rustling path I beat,
The timid hare from its accustom'd seat.
And oh! how sweet this walk o'erhung with wood,
That winds the margin of the solemn flood!
What rural objects steal upon the sight!
What rising views prolong the calm delight!

The brooklet branching from the silver Trent,
The whispering birch by every zephyr bent,
The woody island, and the naked mead,
The lowly hut half hid in groves of reed,
The rural wicket, and the rural stile,
And frequent interspersed, the woodman's pile.
Above, below, where'er I turn my eyes,
Rocks, waters, woods, in grand succession rise.
High up the cliff the varied groves ascend,
And mournful larches o'er the wave impend.
Around, what sounds, what magic sounds arise,
What glimmering scenes salute my ravish'd eyes!
Soft sleep the waters on their pebbly bed,
The woods wave gently o'er my drooping head.
And, swelling slow, comes wafted on the wind,
Lorn Progne's note from distant copse behind.
Still every rising sound of calm delight
Stamps but the fearful silence of the night,
Save when is heard between each dreary rest,
Discordant from her solitary nest,
The owl, dull screaming to the wandering moon;
Now riding, cloud-wrapp'd, near her highest noon:
Or when the wild duck, southering, hither rides,
And plunges, sullen in the sounding tides.

How oft, in this sequester'd spot, when youth
Gave to each tale the holy force of truth,
Have I long linger'd, while the milkmaid sung
The tragic legend, till the woodland rung!
That tale, so sad! which, still to memory dear,
From its sweet source can call the sacred tear,
And (lull'd to rest stern Reason's harsh control)
Steal its soft magic to the passive soul.
These hallow'd shades,—these trees that woo the wind,

Recall its faintest features to my mind.
A hundred passing years, with march sublime,
Have swept beneath the silent wing of time,
Since, in yon hamlet's solitary shade,
Reclusely dwelt the far famed Clifton Maid,
The beauteous Margaret; for her each swain
Confess'd in private his peculiar pain,
In secret sigh'd, a victim to despair,
Nor dared to hope to win the peerless fair.
No more the Shepherd on the blooming mead
Attuned to gaiety his artless reed,
No more entwined the pansied wreath, to deck
His favourite wether's unpolluted neck,
But listless, by yon bubbling stream reclined,
He mix'd his sobbings with the passing wind,
Bemoan'd his hapless love; or, boldly bent,
Far from these smiling fields a rover went,
O'er distant lands, in search of ease, to roam,
A self-will'd exile from his native home.

Yet not to all the maid express'd disdain;
Her Bateman loved, nor loved the youth in vain.
Full oft, low whispering o'er these arching boughs,
The echoing vault responded to their vows,
As here deep hidden from the glare of day,
Enamour'd oft, they took their secret way.

Yon bosky dingle, still the rustics name;
'Twas there the blushing maid confessed her flame.
Down yon green lane they oft were seen to hie,
When evening slumber'd on the western sky.
That blasted yew, that mouldering walnut bare.
Each bears mementos of the fated pair.

One eve, when Autumn loaded every breeze
With the fallen honours of the mourning trees,
The maiden waited at the accustom'd bower.
And waited long beyond the appointed hour,
Yet Bateman came not;—o'er the woodland drear,
Howling portentous did the winds career;
And bleak and dismal on the leafless woods
The fitful rains rush'd down in sullen floods;
The night was dark; as, now and then, the gale
Paused for a moment-Margaret listen'd pale;
But through the covert to her anxious ear
No rustling footstep spoke her lover near.
Strange fears now fill'd her breast,—she knew not why,
She sigh'd, and Bateman's name was in each sigh.
She hears a noise,—'tis he,—he comes at last,—
Alas! 'twas but the gale which hurried past:
But now she hears a quickening footstep sound,
Lightly it comes, and nearer does it bound;
'Tis Bateman's self,—he springs into her arms,

'Tis is he that clasps, and chides her vain alarms.
'Yet why this silence?—I have waited long,
And the cold storm has yell'd the trees among.

And now thou'rt here my fears are fled—yet speak,
Why does the salt tear moisten on thy cheek?
Say, what is wrong?' Now through a parting cloud
The pale moon peer'd from her tempestuous shroud,
And Bateman's face was seen; 'twas deadly white,
And sorrow seem'd to sicken in his sight.
'Oh, speak! my love!' again the maid conjured,
'Why is thy heart in sullen woe immured?'
He raised his head, and thrice essay'd to tell,
Thrice from his lips the unfinished accents fell;
When thus at last reluctantly he broke
His boding silence, and the maid bespoke:
'Grieve not, my love, but ere the morn advance
I on these fields must cast my parting glance;
For three long years, by cruel fate's command,
I go to languish in a foreign land.
Oh, Margaret! omens dire have met my view,
Say, when far distant, wilt thou bear me true?
Should honours tempt thee, and should riches fee,
Wouldst thou forget thine ardent vows to me,
And on the silken couch of wealth reclined,
Banish thy faithful Bateman from thy mind?'

'Oh! why,' replies the maid, 'my faith thus prove,
Canst thou! ah, canst thou, then suspect my love?
Hear me, just God! if from my traitorous heart
My Bateman's fond remembrance e'er shall part,
If, when he hail again his native shore,
He finds his Margaret true to him no more,
May fiends of hell, and every power of dread,
Conjoin'd then drag me from my perjured bed,
And hurl me headlong down these awful steeps,
To find deserved death in yonder deeps!'[2]
Thus spake the maid, and from her finger drew
A golden ring, and broke it quick in two;
One half she in her lovely bosom hides,
The other, trembling, to her love confides.
'This bind the vow,' she said, 'this mystic charm
No future recantation can disarm,
The right vindictive does the fates involve,
No tears can move it, no regrets dissolve.'

She ceased. The death-bird gave a dismal cry,
The river moan'd, the wild gale whistled by,
And once again the lady of the night
Behind a heavy cloud withdrew her light.
Trembling she view'd these portents with dismay;
But gently Bateman kiss'd her fears away:
Yet still he felt conceal'd a secret smart,
Still melancholy bodings fill'd his heart.

When to the distant land the youth was sped,
A lonely life the moody maiden led.
Still would she trace each dear, each well known walk,
Still by the moonlight to her love would talk,
And fancy, as she paced among the trees,
She heard his whispers in the dying breeze.

Thus two years glided on in silent grief;
The third her bosom own'd the kind relief:
Absence had cool'd her love—the impoverish'd flame
Was dwindling fast, when lo! the tempter came;
He offered wealth, and all the joys of life,
And the weak maid became another's wife!
Six guilty months had mark'd the false one's crime,
When Bateman hail'd once more his native clime.
Sure of her constancy, elate he came,
The lovely partner of his soul to claim;
Light was his heart, as up the well known way
He bent his steps-and all his thoughts were gay.
Oh! who can paint his agonizing throes,
When on his ear the fatal news arose!
Chill'd with amazement,—senseless with the blow,
He stood a marble monument of woe;
Till call'd to all the horrors of despair,
He smote his brow, and tore his horrent hair;
Then rush'd impetuous from the dreadful spot,
And sought those scenes (by memory ne'er forgot),
Those scenes, the witness of their growing flame,
And now like witnesses of Margaret's shame.
'Twas night—he sought the river's lonely shore,
And traced again their former wanderings o'er.
Now on the bank in silent grief he stood,
And gazed intently on the stealing flood,
Death in his mein and madness in his eye,
He watch'd the waters as they murmur'd by;
Bade the base murderess triumph o'er his grave—
Prepared to plunge into the whelming wave.

Yet still he stood irresolutely bent,
Religion sternly stay'd his rash intent.
He knelt.—Cool play'd upon his cheek the wind,
And fann'd the fever of his maddening mind,
The willows waved, the stream it sweetly swept,
The paly moonbeam on its surface slept,
And all was peace;—he felt the general calm
O'er his rack'd bosom shed a genial balm:
When casting far behind his streaming eye,
He saw the Grove,—in fancy saw her lie,
His Margaret, lull'd in Germain's arms to rest,
And all the demon rose within his breast.
Convulsive now, he clench'd his trembling hand,
Cast his dark eye once more upon the land,
Then, at one spring he spurn'd the yielding bank,
And in the calm deceitful current sank.

Sad, on the solitude of night, the sound,
As in the stream he plunged, was heard around:
Then all was still-the wave was rough no more,
The river swept as sweetly as before;
The willows waved, the moonbeams shone serene,
And peace returning brooded o'er the scene.

Now, see upon the perjured fair one hang
Remorse's glooms and never ceasing pang.
Full well she knew, repentant now too late,
She soon must bow beneath the stroke of fate.
But, for the babe she bore beneath her breast,
The offended God prolong'd her life unbless'd.
But fast the fleeting moments roll'd away,
And near and nearer drew the dreaded day;
That day foredoom'd to give her child the light,
And hurl its mother to the shades of night.
The hour arrived, and from the wretched wife
The guiltless baby struggled into life.—
As night drew on, around her bed a band
Of friends and kindred kindly took their stand;
In holy prayer they pass'd the creeping time,
Intent to expiate her awful crime.
Their prayers were fruitless.—As the midnight came
A heavy sleep oppress'd each weary frame.
In vain they strove against the o'erwhelming load,
Some power unseen their drowsy lids bestrode.
They slept till in the blushing eastern sky
The blooming Morning oped her dewy eye;
Then wakening wide they sought the ravish'd bed,
But lo! the hapless Margaret was fled;
And never more the weeping train were doom'd
To view the false one, in the deeps intomb'd.

The neighbouring rustics told that in the night
They heard such screams as froze them with affright;
And many an infant, at its mother's breast,
Started dismay'd, from its unthinking rest.
And even now, upon the heath forlorn,
They show the path down which the fair was borne,
By the fell demons, to the yawning wave,
Her own, and murder'd lover's, mutual grave.

Such is the tale, so sad, to memory dear,
Which oft in youth has charm'd my listening ear,
That tale, which bade me find redoubled sweets
In the drear silence of these dark retreats;
And even now, with melancholy power,

Adds a new pleasure to the lonely hour.
'Mid all the charms by magic Nature given
To this wild spot, this sublunary heaven,
With double joy enthusiast Fancy leans
On the attendant legend of the scenes.
This sheds a fairy lustre on the floods,
And breathes a mellower gloom upon the woods;
This, as the distant cataract swells around,
Gives a romantic cadence to the sound;
This, and the deepening glen, the alley green,
The silver stream, with sedgy tufts between,
The massy rock, the wood-encompass'd leas,
The broom-clad islands, and the nodding trees,
The lengthening vista, and the present gloom,
The verdant pathway breathing waste perfume:
These are thy charms, the joys which these impart
Bind thee, bless'd Clifton! close around my heart.

Dear Native Grove! where'er my devious track,
To thee will Memory lead the wanderer back.
Whether in Arno's polish'd vales I stray,
Or where 'Oswego's' swamps obstruct the day;
Or wander lone, where, wildering and wide,
The tumbling torrent laves St. Gothard's side;
Or by old Tejo's classic margent muse,
Or stand entranced with Pyrenean views;
Still, still to thee, where'er my footsteps roam,
My heart shall point, and lead the wanderer home.
When Splendour offers, and when Fame incites,
I'll pause, and think of all thy dear delights,
Reject the boon, and, wearied with the change,
Renounce the wish which first induced to range;
Turn to these scenes, these well known scenes once more,
Trace once again old Trent's romantic shore,
And tired with worlds, and all their busy ways,
Here waste the little remnant of my days.
But if the Fates should this last wish deny,
And doom me on some foreign shore to die;
Oh! should it please the world's supernal King,
That weltering waves my funeral dirge shall sing;
Or that my corse should, on some desert strand,
Lie stretch'd beneath the Simoom's blasting hand;
Still, though unwept I find a stranger tomb,
My sprite shall wander through this favourite gloom,
Ride on the wind that sweeps the leafless grove,
Sigh on the wood-blast of the dark alcove,
Sit a lorn spectre on yon well known grave,
And mix its moanings with the desert wave.

Thus we are transported into the romance, which appears so similar to Cathy and Heathcliff's love story in its foundations, until the lovers meet their end in a "mutual grave" (l.440). It is on this line that the second scrawl lines appear, at the very termination of this stanza. Essentially, the Brontë symbols clearly designate where the intimate love story of Margaret and Bateman begins and ends. Until this moment, Kirke White has been more engrossed in the natural elements of the grove where these lovers would meet. Before he even mentions the folktale of the Clifton Maid, we are introduced to the pastoral imagery of the area, as one would expect of a poet of Kirke White's Romantic generation. He imagines himself wandering lonely as the cloud-like Wordsworth, through this area of local beauty:

> *Here lonely wandering o'er the sylvan bower*
> *I come to pass the meditative hour*
> (ll.29-30)

He recalls the finer details of this grove, increasing the lucidity of his memory, imagining himself walking along the wide, grass lane, finding himself on the south bank of the River Trent, as was the common path for locals:

> *...from the silver Trent,*
> *The whispering birch by every zephyr bent,*
> *The woody island, and the naked mead,*
> *The lowly hut half hid in groves of reed,*
> (ll.215-218)

His unbroken descriptions and steady rhythm allows the poem to mimic the flow of the river and absorbs Kirke White and his readers deeper into the fantasy. In exercising his own poetic practice for describing rustic beauty, Kirke White is, in fact, searching for that entity which has eluded many a poet: inspiration.

Although Emily, herself, would struggle with writer's block – and her own poetry became renowned for her Romantic imagery – she,

Engraving of Clifton Grove which appears in the *Remains*.

or one of her siblings, mark the love story, making it possible
to circumvent Kirke White's lofty images and cut straight to the
romance. Emily's dissatisfaction with Patrick concerning the story
of his relationship with Maria meant that she was eager to better
comprehend the power of romantic passion and the fervency that
would create such vivid images in Patrick's own poetry. However,
when she cannot trace her father's love story, she goes in search
of another. Thus, in Kirke White, she finds the Virgil to her Dante,
leading her through the mind's complex forests to the core of the
romance fiction.

The Nottingham town of Clifton, to all appearances, has always
seemed a pleasant and unassuming settlement, and yet the legends
of its residents, as Kirke White describes, often:

> *draws (the local's) household round their evening fire,*
> *And tell(s) the oft-told tales that never tire*
> (ll.17-18)

This spans from the tale of the "Clifton Maid" which would influence Kirke White and Emily Brontë's writings, to its brave knights, among whom is a figure reminiscent of Bluebeard: Sir Gervase Clifton (1587-1666). Known locally by Clifton residents as "Sir Gervase with the seven wives", he appears to be a "black widower" of sorts. All of his wives met a premature end, the sixth of whom was born a Miss Jane Eyre, daughter of Anthony Eyre. In the roles of knights and burgesses, the Eyres, Cliftons and even the family of "White" are integrated throughout Clifton's history, as *Thomas Bailey's Annals of Nottinghamshire* illuminates. One legend Bailey speaks of is a duel between a Tory and a Whig in the early seventeenth century. One of the supporters of the Tory champion was a Vincent Eyre, owner of the town's needle factory, a detail which recalls Mr Olivier, father of Rosamund in *Jane Eyre*.

While we are given the impression it was Clifton's history which appealed to Charlotte, it is its folktales which struck Emily, unsurprisingly for an author who incorporates "old wives' tales" into her novel. Through the unworldly Nelly Dean, the Heights' inhabitants are taught songs and lore, one instance being her recital of *Fairy Annie's Wedding*, although frequently interrupted by the pious Joseph who believes the story of magic to be wicked and blasphemous (257). Her action, therefore, of recounting the story of Cathy and Heathcliff places their romance among the other local stories in her repertoire, although the locals of her story have not yet come to idealise their "romance" as those of Clifton with Margaret and Bateman's "tale, so sad" (l.243). Clifton Grove is integrated firmly in the psyche of its natives, as Nottingham historian, Frank E. Earp, illustrates: "(h)ow many people of my generation have fond memories of Clifton Grove? [...] 'Down the Witches Steps!' is still a popular saying among Clifton folk" (Earp, 'Clifton Grove'), the Witches Steps being a local name for an incline within the trees which line the grove's path either side.

Kirke White and his contemporaries believed the area to be

steeped in an indefinable mystic power, of which Emily Brontë's Joseph would never have approved:

> *Mid all the charms by magic nature given*
> *To this wild spot sheds … a fairy lustre*
> (ll.447-448; l.451)

As Kirke White's recollections grow increasingly vivid, a concentric narrative structure commences: Kirke White's true self, in search of a muse, imagines himself in Clifton. This extension of himself wanders the path and hears the folk-tales of the "neighbouring rustics" (l.433) and hears how the:

> "… milkmaid sung
> *The tragic legend, till the woodland rung*"
> (l.241-242).

Thus the poem progresses into the integral romance flagged by the Brontë scribbles.

The construction of *Wuthering Heights* parallels this layered style, with the stranger, Lockwood, being told the story of Cathy and Heathcliff by witness, Nelly Dean, but not before he has been given some basic insight into the tale from Cathy's book and her ghosts. Equally, Kirke White never experiences the love story directly. His information, like Lockwood's, is built upon his own imagination and intergenerational stories. Fiction and the memories of others are as woven into *Clifton Grove* as they were in Emily's own knowledge of her mother. The multiple narrative layers of *Wuthering Heights* represent the boundaries between Emily's story and Maria's, consequently she responds to Kirke White's gradations of storytelling.

The role of memory is significant in both texts. Nelly's recollections, as well as relics from Cathy's childhood, are the driving force of *Wuthering Heights'* core narrative. Similarly, in recalling the grove and its folklore, Kirke White is breathing life into its legacy. Memories fuel imagination for both Emily Brontë and Kirke White, and this subtext is fuelled further by *Wuthering Heights's* meta-literary structure. Cathy preserves her journal in published books, detailing scenarios imagined by Emily, inspired by her own family's childhood marginalia in *The Remains of Henry Kirke White* and *Poetical Works*. As Lockwood recites these memories, Cathy returns to reclaim the space and materials of her childhood.

However, this is not the sole instance of Cathy wishing to relive her youth. The character's delirium is notorious, the absence or neglect of Heathcliff causes her to call his name across the moors; a popular scene in adaptation, often misattributed to the novel. In one such state of restlessness, induced by Heathcliff's apparent preference for her sister-in-law, Isabella, Nelly observes her to be in "feverish bewilderment" (101). Cathy's disorientation appears to mimic, or rather foreshadow, Lockwood's state of mind on the appearance of her spectre. As Lockwood cannot distinguish poltergeists from dreams, memories from imagination, Cathy also seems to experience a sleep-induced haunting: "Don't you see that face?", she asks Nelly, only for Emily to reveal that Cathy is simply staring into a mirror. (103). Haunted by her own image, she cannot distinguish her dream-self from reality, much as Kirke White amalgamates his "memory" self in Clifton with the "poet" self in his office. Cathy yearns to regress to the simplicity of childhood, much as Kirke White does: "I wish I were out of doors! I wish I were a girl again […] laughing at my injuries, not maddening under them!" (105). She begs the window open, as her ghost did at the commencement of the narrative, as if the glass acts as a barrier between time. (105). Breathing in the moor's air she believes herself "a stranger: an exile, and outcast" (105), imitating the "self-will'd exile" (l.266) that is Kirke White.

The opening of the barrier between place-memory and reality is mimicked by Kirke White's method of remembrance. Kirke White imagines how the "'nighted rustic late" swings his "jarring gate" (l.12), welcoming him back to his childhood home. Equally, Cathy imagines she can see Joseph's lantern, "(h)e's waiting till I come home that he may lock the gate." (105). As she imagines herself crossing this space, she braves the "ghosts" of Gimmerton Kirk, as Kirke White does those of Clifton, eagerly submersing herself in her own thoughts. She yearns to be in her own bed "in the old house" with the "wind sounding in the firs by the lattice" (103), just as the branches tap against the window before the ghost's face appears to Lockwood.

Once again, the box bed represents an in-between amid life and afterlife, a catalyst for fiction, just as Kirke White submerses himself beyond the gates of Clifton in order to grant himself poetic inspiration. Suddenly the gate-like drawing, which marked the story's progress into the tale of Margaret and Bateman, seems a premonition of the peripheries which fill *Wuthering Heights* – Lockwood's first introduction to the love story of the Heights occurs once he dares to pass the gate of the Heights: "The 'walk in'", spoken by Joseph, "was uttered with closed teeth, and expressed the sentiment 'Go to the Deuce': even the gate over which he leant manifested no sympathising movement" (1).

By the same token, the final close of the Heights's gate seems a parallel of the second sketch, which denotes the love story's conclusion. Lockwood deliberates the "country folks" protestations which state "if you asked them, would swear on their bible that he (Heathcliff) walks. […] that old man by the kitchen fire affirms he has seen two on 'em looking out of his chamber window" (280). Equally, the milk-maids of Clifton grove claim to see the star-crossed lovers "hallow'd shades" (l.237), as Lockwood meets with a shepherd boy who claims to see Heathcliff and "a woman" upon the moor (281). Moreover, Kirke White's "neighbouring rustics" (l.433) claim to hear Margaret's cries "even now, upon the heath forlorn" (l.437) and share their experiences around the fireside. Further parallels are drawn between the uproar of the locals of *Wuthering Heights* that Heathcliff's last wishes for burial are adhered to. Concerning his desecration of Cathy's grave, Heathcliff expresses his plan: having struck one side of the coffin loose, he bribes the sexton to "slide" one side of his own coffin free, as he once slid open the panels of the box bed in the hopes of reuniting with Cathy's spirit.

So when Heathcliff is buried, he and Cathy share not just a grave, but a coffin (240). Equally, following Bateman's death, Margaret drags herself to the place in the grove where the self-destruction occurred so that she may die beside him: "Her own, and murder'd lover's, mutual grave" (l.440). However, it is in death, and the circumstances leading to their tragic fate, where the similarities between Kirke White and Emily Brontë's lovers end. When Heathcliff returns from his three-year absence from Yorkshire, he is a wealthy man, the source of his fortune unsettlingly vague. He is aware that Cathy has married Edgar Linton, and fails to feign a preference for revenge over reunion: "(Catherine) kept her gaze fixed on him as if she feared he would vanish were she to remove it. He (Heathcliff) did not raise his to her often [...] each time more confidently, [with] undisguised delight" (79).

Nevertheless, he marries Isabella and drags Hindley into ruin, all the while mentally torturing Cathy from this combination of disregard and persecution. Ultimately, she dies in childbirth: "About twelve o'clock that night was born the (second) Catherine [...] and two hours after the mother died, having never recovered sufficient consciousness to miss Heathcliff, or know Edgar" (137). Bateman, however, returns once "(s)ix guilty months" (l.361) marked his Margaret's wedding to the prosperous, Germain, instead of the afore expected three years (see l.315). Presuming Margaret to have been true to her promises of faithfulness:

> ... elate he came,
> *The lovely partner of his soul to claim*
> (ll.363-364)

On learning of her marriage, Bateman returns to their former haunt, the grove, much as Heathcliff returns to Wuthering Heights, however his revenge is much more directly psychological. Bateman enters the grove with the intention of taking his own life – to make the townsfolk "witnesses of Margaret's shame" (l.376). Whereas Heathcliff implores the return of Cathy's ghost with the cry: "You said I killed you – haunt me, then!" (140). Bateman moments before his suicide "(b)ade the base murderess triumph o'er his grave" (l.383), subverting the gender of the "killer". Although Cathy threatens to die if Heathcliff leaves her again as she lays upon her deathbed: "I shall die!" (136), and previously threatened: "I'd kill myself directly!" (101), her death reads as an unwillingness to recover from childbirth and delirium rather than Bateman's premeditated drowning.

While a feminist reader might interpret this gender-inversion as Emily Brontë compelling the man to consider his role in the death of a woman, a psychological perspective might consider her constant exposure to Patrick's grief over Maria. Regardless of the preferred interpretation, Emily does not completely interchange the hero's fate for the heroine's. While Bateman casts himself into "the calm, deceitful current" (l.400) of the river, Heathcliff also meets his fate in his and Cathy's former sanctuary: the box bed. Lockwood peeks between the bed's panels to find Heathcliff seeming "to smile", observing "his face and throat were washed with rain; the bed-clothes dripped, and he was perfectly still" (279). His drenched state, as a result of the rain, mimics the submersion of Bateman into the river, as Heathcliff also invites Cathy to witness his death: the lattice where her ghost appeared to Lockwood: "flapping to and fro, had grazed one hand that rested on the sill; no blood trickled from the broken skin" (279). Where Cathy's incorporeal ghost did bleed after being cut on the glass, the mortal Heathcliff does not. Where memory gave the spirit an earthly presence, it causes Heathcliff to transcend human injury, once again emphasising the assimilation of the natural and the supernatural this box bed facilitates.

The locals question whether Heathcliff intended to commit

suicide, although he denied himself food and drink in the days leading up to this event, yet the eerie peacefulness of this "sinful" death is reminiscent of Bateman's acceptance of his fate. Equally, Bateman summons his lover's image: "in fancy he saw her lie" (l.394) in the grove, their sacred place, but in his mind she is "lull'd in Germain's arms" (l.395), just as Cathy's ghost addresses herself as Edgar's wife, "Catherine Linton", rather than Heathcliff's lover (20).

This subtext of a loved and vital person that cannot be owned is one which may have spoken to the motherless Emily. Consequently, motherhood is a fleeting state of being in *Wuthering Heights*, as in *Clifton Grove*. While Kirke White appears to have had a close connection with his mother, with much of his correspondence preserved by Southey in the *Remains* being addressed to her, the Margaret of Clifton folklore does not live to know her child. With Bateman's curse prolonged long enough solely for the "dreaded day" (l.414), the child is born and the mother is hurled into "shades of night" (l.416). When the hour arrives – exactly midnight (l.423), as with the birth of the second Catherine in *Wuthering Heights* (137) – that the "guiltless baby struggled into life" (l.418). Margaret does not die instantly, unlike the almost immediate death of Cathy. Instead, Margaret waits until those who are keeping watch over her, fearing that her inconstancy will result in her end, fall asleep. When they wake up, Margaret is nowhere to be seen: "the hapless Margaret was fled" (l.430).

Kirke White ends the story by describing how the Clifton locals swear to have seen Margaret, in life and death, to have made her way to the grove, where she and Bateman sleep in the "mutual grave" (l.440), insinuating she, too, threw herself into the river. Once more, the lovers' genders are inverted so it is Heathcliff, not Cathy, who mimics Margaret's desire to rejoin her lover in death. Margaret, however, only waits until her child is born to reunite with Bateman in the afterlife, where Heathcliff continues to survive for decades after Cathy's demise.

Emily forces the lovers to live separately to accentuate the power of the "literary limbo" where Cathy's ghost haunts not only the locals, but Heathcliff himself, mimicking the prolonged absence of Maria's direct influence upon the Parsonage. As Kirke White contemplates the fate of his lovers, the second Brontë marker rests beside this line – just as the Heights's garden gates closes as Lockwood and Nelly discuss the burial of Heathcliff "as he had wished" (281), signifying the beginning and the end of both stories.

Clifton Grove's ghostly imagery had an evident affect upon Emily Brontë's gothic masterpiece, yet while the spiritual romance of Kirke White's verse inspired the foundation of Emily's story, it was her own capabilities and intrinsic psychology that allowed her to expand upon his imagery. Kirke White's meta-lore is transformed into a nuanced narrative, stripping back some of the romance so we may consider its ripple effect upon future generations. While Emily's desire for a link to the past led her to peruse her mother's edition of *The Remains of Henry Kirke White*, his *Clifton Grove* – and the search it depicts for any form of interaction with a past romance – was a sentiment she knew all too well. This tale of never wishing to be separated from a loved one spoke to the motherless Brontë children; their mother's relics may have been inspiring in literary terms, but it was a poor emotional substitute for the lack of their own memories. Kirke White had the memories of his native grove, yet the stories contained there were largely unobtainable, relying upon folktales and the recollections of his elders to breathe life into this story from his childhood.

Mimicking Kirke White, as she once did her father, Emily asks us how it must feel when the tale we are trying to retrieve is a childhood itself, a childhood before the death of her mother when she was left with nothing but literary memoranda. Thus, Maria haunts the pages of *Wuthering Heights* as Cathy does its eponymous homestead. Like Cathy's ghost, she is an amalgamation of different times and perceptions, as Lockwood describes: although the ghost identifies herself as "Catherine Linton", her married name, despite him having read her maiden name Earnshaw "twenty times for Linton" (20). Moreover, he describes the ghost as having the face of a child, in spite of her apparently adult status. With no discernible age, this spirit appears an amalgamation of time itself, a "dreadful collection of memoranda" from moments in Cathy's life.

In this eternalist reading, Emily is embodying her frustration that she must rely on the words and memories of others to create a picture of her mother, echoed in the structures of her own and Kirke White's tales of ghosts. The *Remains* itself, having travelled from her home town in Cornwall, is a relic of a period before Maria became a wife and parent, therefore to claim it was a vestige of a "mother" was as ungraspable as a ghost for Emily, forcing a married name on a single woman. However, if she was forced to rely on the words of others to breathe life back into her mother, Emily would infuse Kirke White's imagery with her own spirit so her imagination, and the memory of Maria, could create a reimagined, learned heaven they could share, with Kirke White as their guide.

In the in-betweens of beds and books, Emily chooses to believe Maria's literary vestiges – and her own creative prowess – had the power to make Maria's memory manifest, demanding entrance to the Parsonage.

Works Cited:

Bailey, Thomas. *Annals of Nottinghamshire: History of the County of Nottingham, including the borough* Vol.III. (London: Simpkin, Marshall, and Co., 1853)

Barker, Juliet. *The Brontës: A Life in Letters*. (London: Viking, 1997)

Brontë, Emily. *The Complete Poems*. Ed. Janet Gezari. (London: Penguin Books, Ltd. 1992)

Brontë, Emily and Anne Brontë. *Wuthering Heights & Agnes Grey*. (London: Smith, Elder & Co., 1870)

Brontë, Patrick. *Brontëana: The Rev. Patrick Brontë, A.B., His Collected Works and Life*. (Bingley: T. Harrison & Sons, 1898)

Du Maurier, Daphne. *Vanishing Cornwall*. (Cornwall: Doubleday, 1967)

Earp, Frank E. 'Clifton Grove', *nottinghamhiddenhistoryteam*, 2013, <https://nottinghamhiddenhistoryteam.wordpress.com/2013/03/11/clifton-grove/>

Earp, Frank E. 'The Fair Maid of Clifton', *nottinghamhiddenhistoryteam*, 2013, <https://nottinghamhiddenhistoryteam.wordpress.com/2013/03/11/the-fair-maid-of-clifton/>

Ellis, Samantha. *Take Courage: Anne Brontë and the Art of Life.* (London: Chatto & Windus, 2017)

Gaskell, Elizabeth. *Life of Charlotte Brontë, Volume One.* (1857) (Reprint: New York: Cosimo, Inc. 2008)

Lutz, Deborah. *The Brontë Cabinet: Three Lives in Nine Objects.* (New York: W. W. Norton, 2016)

White, Henry Kirke. *The Remains of HENRY KIRKE WHITE, of Nottingham, Late of St. John's College, Cambridge; With an Account of his LIFE.* Ed. Robert Southey. Vol. 1. Fourth Edition. (London: Printed for Vernor, Hood, and Sharpe, 1810)

Notes:

1   All subsequent references will be given parenthetically. Citations from this poem are in reference to Volume Two of the Brontë Edition, pp. 11-28.

2   For further reading of "marketing" the love story of *Wuthering Heights*, please refer to Kamilla Elliott. *Rethinking the Novel/Film Debate.* Cambridge: Cambridge University Press, 2003. 'Chapter Five: Literary Cinema and the Form/Content Debate', pp. 133-181.

3   Charlotte Brontë, *The History of the Year*, 12th March 1829, in Juliet Barker, *The Brontës: A Life in Letters* (London: Viking, 1997), pp. 11-12.

4   For further reading please refer to Juliet Barker, *The Brontës* (London: Abacus, 2010), pp. 234-235.

5   Charlotte Brontë letter to Hartley Coleridge, 10th December 1840 in *A Life in Letters*, pp. 85-87.

6   Charlotte Brontë letter to Ellen Nussey, 16th February 1850 in *A Life in Letters*, pp. 266-267.

7   Patrick Brontë, 'Lines, Addressed to a Lady, on her Birth-Day' (pp. 82-85), 'Kirkstall Abbey' (pp. 76-80) in *Brontëana: The Rev. Patrick Brontë, A.B., His Collected Works and Life.* (Bingley: T. Harrison & Sons, 1898)

8   Emily Brontë, 'Written in Aspin Castle', pp. 139-142, in *The Complete Poems.* Ed. Janet Gezari. (London: Penguin Books, Ltd. 1992)

9   Patrick Brontë, 'Verses, Sent to a Lady on her Birth-Day' in *Brontëana*, pp. 44-45.

10 For further reading, please refer to Frank E. Earp's 'The Fair Maid of Clifton', *nottinghamhiddenhistoryteam*, 2013, https://nottinghamhiddenhistoryteam.wordpress.com/2013/03/11/the-fair-maid-of-clifton/

    For further reading, please refer to Thomas Bailey's *Annals of Nottinghamshire: History of the County of Nottingham, including the borough* Vol.III. (London: Simpkin, Marshall, and Co., 1853)

THE BRONTË SOCIETY

Bringing the Brontës to the world and the world to Yorkshire

One of the world's oldest literary societies, the Brontë Society was founded in 1893 to organise a permanent home for items belonging to the Brontë family.

Today, the Brontë Society is a global, multi-faceted organisation with a mission to celebrate the lives and works of the Brontës, maintaining their legacy and contemporary significance to a global audience. It runs the world-famous accredited Brontë Parsonage Museum in Haworth, which houses the world's largest collection of Brontë manuscripts, furniture and personal possessions. It conserves, interprets, displays and builds creative engagement with its unique collection and the landscape that inspired the Brontës; it furthers scholarship and better understanding of their lives and works.

In addition to an award-winning learning offer, the Society delivers a contemporary arts programme which engages with and interrogates the collection in innovative ways. Taking its cue from the Brontës' own multidisciplinary approach, the Society explores Brontë links with literature and other artforms through partnerships, finding new ways to see and work with the collection.

The Brontë Society's commercial arm, Brontë Genius, runs the museum's shop, the profits from which help preserve the museum and its collection. You can browse the shop's wide range of books, homeware and literary gifts at **www.bronte.org.uk/bronte-shop**.

You can also support the work of the Society by joining the growing global membership. More information can be found at **www.bronte.org.uk/support-us**.